COPING IN THE 80s
Eliminating Needless
Stress and Guilt

COPING IN THE 80s Eliminating Needless Stress and Guilt

Joel Wells

THE THOMAS MORE PRESS
Chicago, Illinois

Acknowledgments:

The author is grateful to the following for permission to include material from:

STRESS AND THE HEALTHY FAMILY, © 1985 by Dolores Curran. Published by the Winston Press, Minneapolis, Minnesota. All rights reserved. Used with permission.

YOUR AGING PARENTS, © 1985 by John Deedy. Published by the Thomas More Press, 223 West Erie St., Chicago, Illinois 60610. Used with permission.

T. H. Holmes, and R. H. Rahe, "The Social Readjustment Rating Scale," *Journal of Psychosomatic Research* 11:213-218, 1967. Used with permission of the authors. © 1967, Pergamon Press, LTD.

THE STRESS OF LIFE, © 1956, 1976 by Hans Selye. Published by the McGraw-Hill Book Company, New York, New York. Used by permission of the publisher.

Hardcover ISBN 0-88347-201-5
Paperback ISBN 0-88347-202-3

Contents

HOW I RELAX

"In the light of research on stress, my advice would be:

Fight for your highest attainable aim
but never put up resistance in vain.

There is no ready-made success formula which will suit everybody. We are all different. But, since humans are essentially rational beings, the better we know what makes us tick, the more likely we will be to make a success of life. Our ultimate aim is to express ourselves as fully as possible, according to our own lights."

Hans Seyle, M.D.
The Stress of Life

INTRODUCTION

STRESS, which is any disturbance, strain, stimulus or interference that upsets the functioning of mind or body, is as old as humankind itself. Guilt makes its first recorded debut in the book of Genesis when, after eating of the apple plucked from the tree of knowledge of good and evil, Adam and Eve felt shame in discovering their nakedness: "so they stitched fig leaves together and made themselves loin cloths."

Stress and guilt have been with us ever since.

Nothing so deeply seated in human physiology and consciousness is ever going to disappear. Stress and guilt are a natural, even necessary part of living. Each plays an essential role in our behavior. Stress triggers one of the most basic reactions necessary for survival—the signal to fight or escape. It also provides the impetus to face up to challenges, compete and achieve something. Guilt brings a moral dimension to human life that separates it from bestial indifference to the consequences of killing or otherwise harming ourselves and our fellow creatures in wanton fashion.

But, because failure to cope with prolonged "disstress" causes not only anxiety and depression which paralyze our minds, but also destroys health and wellbeing, and because guilt is in reality a powerful form of internal stress which rises out of our consciences and consciousness, we have to learn to cope with both.

It is the thesis of this book that the times we live in have multiplied the causes, varieties and pervasiveness of stress and guilt to a dangerous degree. We shall never be free of either, but it is possible, through understanding and by taking certain positive steps and adopting certain attitudes, to eliminate huge amounts of needless stress and guilt which afflict our lives and the lives of those we love. As Dr. Barbara Brown puts it in her book *Between Health & Illness:* "Stress is a phenomenon generated almost exclusively by society's mad pace of the twentieth century. Diminished well-being is the social Pac-Man that devours coping and psychic energy and inner strength. Before it wins the game of our lives, it needs some serious, sober attention."

No one sets out on an extended trip without carrying some luggage. But, as every experienced traveler knows, nothing can spoil what might otherwise be a very pleasant and rewarding journey than having to lug an excessive number of bags and suitcases every step of the way.

No one should expect to negotiate the journey of life without a certain amount of stress and guilt. But it's not pleasant nor is it necessary to be burdened down with constant and oppressive amounts of either.

Millions of us cope with what the "father" of stress research, Dr. Hans Selye, has called "the stress of life." Both to make this book less abstract and also to provide some living examples of how real people manage their own "stress of life," I asked a number of people in widely varying positions, occupations and lifestyles, if they had any special routines, rituals or "tricks" which they used to help themselves relax, to interrupt or put aside the tensions of the day.

I am extremely grateful to all who responded and you will find their helpful replies interspersed throughout the pages that follow.

Joel Wells

CHAPTER ONE
Guilt

LIKE murder, guilt is a loaded word. It carries a built-in judgment. If I've killed someone it may have been by accident, perhaps in self-defense, or in the course of military action. But if I've murdered someone, I've committed a deliberate crime.

Just so with guilt. If I've done, or failed to do, something that leaves me wondering about the correctness of my behavior, that's one thing; if I feel guilty about something I did or failed to do, then I have already convinced myself that my behavior was unquestionably wrong. Only the law can convict a person of murder. Anyone can convict themselves of guilt.

Guilt has no pleasant associations. *Webster's Collegiate Thesaurus* lists its synonyms as "blame, culpability, fault, onus." It's true that guilt can spur a person to positive action: I will reform; I will not make that mistake again; I will apologize and make it up to her; I will make better use of my time and talents; I will think before I talk; I will never strike the child again, etc. But it's also true that guilt can bring on feelings of inadequacy, low self-esteem, worry, depression and even the urge for self-punishment and suicide.

That is because guilt is a form of stress. It is not a stressor in the technical sense—some disturbance, frustration, or obstacle that, depending on how we interpret and inter-act with it may, or may not, trigger the stress syndrome. Guilt is, as noted, a loaded word: if one feels guilty then the judgment has already been handed down. Guilt always produces stress; the more serious or basic or central to our self-image, the more serious and long-lasting the stress.

As must always be the case with true stress, as opposed to shock or pain, there is nothing physical about guilt. It is purely subjective, rising out of our own mind. We commonly say that somebody else makes us feel guilty, but in reality we make ourselves feel guilty through some self-established method of comparison which finds us wanting. But the fact that it is subjective rather than physical doesn't make guilt and the stress it produces any less real. It only makes it harder to deal with.

Wherefore Guilt

Even though none of us can remember the blissful moment, we are not born feeling guilty about anything. There is no guilt whatsoever in babies. Guilt is acquired, absorbed, learned and accumulated as we grow up. Guilt is as necessary as it is inescapable. Necessary because it is part of the moral dimension that is the mystery of being human. Animals simply do not experience guilt. Domestic animals have been trained and bred to be less "savage" than their wild counterparts. But nature is "red in tooth and claw"; the cheetah feels no remorse over killing the zebra, nor does the eagle feel ashamed when it rends the rabbit's throat. Some dog lovers will swear that Rover knows when he's done something naughty and feels guilty and acts ashamed. He may know that he's transgressed a rule, all right, but it's not guilt that makes

HOW I RELAX

I suppose my chief coping mechanism is humor. I tend to joke about—well, almost everything, come to think about it.

Another method I've used, for years, in coping with stress, is to use a device called a slant board or reclining board.

One lies on it with the head in the lower position and the feet elevated.

I generally increase the angle of elevation by positioning the board so that I can rest my feet—as high as possible—on a table top, bookshelf or wall surface.

Even five or ten minutes in that position, eyes closed, is helpful in recharging my energies. If I can spend half an hour or so in such a position, I am remarkably refreshed.

This works not because of the faith one might have in its efficacy, but for purely physical reasons. First of all, one is lying down, which is always restful. Secondly, the angle greatly increases the flow of blood to the brain. I assume this is the chief reason for the energy increase.

Steve Allen
Composer, Musician,
Author, Actor
Entertainer

him quiver, but anticipation and fear of direct physical punishment. He has convicted himself of nothing.

By whatever name one cares to call it—moral faculty, conscience—there is a dimension of human nature that measures right from wrong. There is also a sort of grand moral consensus that certain behavior is either right, wrong or neutral. Many philosophers and theologians have envisioned this consensus as a "natural law" which is divinely written into the human moral faculty and which emerges as a sort of basic conscience at the age of reason—the time when a young person is able both to think abstractly and to know right from wrong.

It is not to dispute anyone's religious faith or philosophical convictions to say that this moral consensus has evolved historically and has been greatly influenced by both religious beliefs and social factors. It has varied wildly from tribe to tribe, century to century, place to place, civilization to civilization. There are very few basics, universals, if you will, that have existed always and without change in the history of human morality. Murder would seem to have always been regarded as "most foul," but human sacrifice and ritual killing have flourished, as has cannibalism, incest, polygamy, torture, infanticide and dozens of other things that our contemporary Western consciences find repugnant and evil.

"Respectable," God-fearing men kept slaves with clear consciences in this country until just a bit over a century ago, just as the Egyptians did more than three millenia before them. Those who bewail the "sexual revolution" and modern promiscuity should go back via time machine to the streets of ancient

Rome. Divorce was once the great taboo which could bring down kings and politicians from high station.

The point is not that slavery was once good and now is bad; or that divorce was once bad and now is good. Religious belief will always have its right and power to convince its faithful followers of what is good and what is evil—that is, to have a powerful role in the formation of the individual moral faculty. The point is that whether or not something is objectively good or bad is, in practice, secondary to what the individual has in fact perceived it to be. If she perceives something to be evil, or bad, or just plain wrong, and does it anyway; if he perceives something as good, desirable or simply that which should be done, and fails to do it—then both she and he will feel guilty.

In order to eliminate unnecessary guilt, then, it is imperative to realize that people can acquire standards that make them feel guilty about virtually anything, provided that is what they have been taught to regard as good or evil, regardless of whether or not it really is, or whether people of other moral persuasions regard it in a different way.

Given the opportunity and the perverse will to do so, it is quite easy to convince a child that "stepping on a crack will break your mother's back." Experience will soon teach the child this is not really true, but that will not prevent a wrenching twinge of guilt between the time when, still angry from a maternal correction, he deliberately steps on every crack he can spot on his way home from school and the absolution of being greeted at the kitchen door by a thoroughly erect and mobile mom.

And we are not speaking here only of major moral

issues, of murder, rape and child abuse. Guilt of the
sort that most modern stress is made of walks far less
dramatic paths. We are all different, and all of us feel
guilty about different things because all of us have
been differently conditioned by a host of factors—the
ethnic and religious traditions of our parents and extended family, by the mores and standards of the society and culture around us, by playmates, teachers,
peer groups, even by sexual role models.

Reassessing Guilt—Sorting Things Out

Good and evil may be absolutes, but as we have
seen, guilt is a moveable feast of self-accusation. Some
people experience strong and enduring guilt about doing or not doing something which doesn't cause others
a moment's concern. American Catholics used to feel
guilty if they ate meat on Friday, a matter of absolutely
no concern to their fellow citizens. Some people feel
guilty about cheating on their income taxes; others
feel no compunction, other than the fear of being
caught in the act. Millions still experience guilt when
they tell a lie, besmirch a reputation, take God's name
"in vain," look at pornography, spank their children,
work on the Sabbath, steal something from the office
or factory, cut classes, eat between meals, have an af-
fair, or even jaywalk; other millions do all these things
routinely without a second thought.

Another consideration worth noting is that what
people feel guilty about is not immutable, it can and
does change in the course of a lifetime. This may be
more true today than it was in the past because of the

rapidity of change and the knowledge or information explosion which has let us experience, at least vicariously, the way other people think and behave while at the same time further conditioning us with new knowledge and values. (Going back to our American Catholics for a moment, their guilt about eating meat on Friday is no more because the Church law requiring weekly abstinence was abolished. More than a few Catholics wondered to what department in heaven or hell their former guilt had been consigned.)

New knowledge can cause critical thinking which may free people from past guilt feelings. It can also add new ones. Not many years ago most smokers puffed away with impunity; now a great many who continue smoking feel guilty not only about what they are doing to their own health, but also about the displeasure and disgust of those around them. (And sometimes the touching concern, as witnessed by the recent story of a California girl who refused to agree to a life-saving heart transplant for herself until her parents signed an oath that they would quit cigarettes for good.)

New medical knowledge, together with its widespread dissemination by the media, has made Americans more conscious of other health hazards such as hypertension, obesity, drug and alcohol abuse, venereal diseases and AIDS, so that we now have a sort of national guilt trip among those who smoke, drink, eat between meals, fail to jog, eat salt and sugar, engage in promiscuous sex and otherwise flout the new conventional (and in this case, quite accurate) wisdom.

This is one example from among dozens, in which

guilty feelings are not only appropriate but might become a positive spur to behavior modification for the better. *There is no question about it, much guilt is justified, whether or not it leads to altered behavior or attitudes. But it is just as true that much guilt is not justified, either by fact or because it is something totally unnecessary, totally inappropriate, totally outdated, but which has been allowed to fester away for years simply because we picked it up somewhere long ago and far away.*

Inventory Time

It should be more than evident by now, that there is nothing sacred about guilt. It is a form of stress that cannot and should not be altogether eliminated but which can certainly be curtailed and minimized by some therapeutic mental housekeeping. Every adult owes it to herself or himself to make an inventory of the things that cause guilt feelings, and then take a hard-nosed look at all of them with an eye toward consciously getting rid of those which really have no justification.

We have seen that one source of guilt rises out of failure to live up to religious beliefs. I used the example of Catholic guilt about eating meat on Friday not to poke fun at Catholics, but simply to demonstrate that here, as in virtually every other faith, there are some areas, prohibitions, rules and regulations which are less than central to belief and personal holiness. I am in no way advocating religious rebellion when I suggest that many of us place equal moral weight,

HOW I RELAX

I'm afraid the way I deal with stress is not very creative or imaginative. I swim for a mile every morning and then I use self-hypnotism which I learned from Erika Fromm a number of years ago as a technique for meditation and reflection. If that doesn't work I call one of my close friends—a reassuring conversation always helps me to relax.

I also use self-hypnotism (usually after swimming) when I'm searching for an idea for a novel or a story and finally, I use it when I'm travelling or really worn out, to relax. It is merely a technique, much like other forms of meditation, to detach oneself from the noise and confusion in the world and focus deep within oneself on the realities that really matter. By way of generalization, I think I'd say you can't beat meditation for fighting stress.

Bizzarely, that's what they told us in the seminary.

Rev. Andrew M. Greeley
Professor of Sociology
University of Arizona
Best-selling novelist

and thus experience equal guilt, when we harbor major doubts and commit major lapses or sins, as when we ignore, transgress or just plain forget about some highly incidental or historically dubious minor matters.

It is also true that many of the little rules, maxims and taboos of childhood morality and deportment, laid on us at home, in Church, synagogue and Sunday school, are still allowed to add their totally juvenile two-cents worth of guilt to our otherwise adult lives. In this area religious people of all persuasions might do well to heed the advice of Saint Paul: "When I was a child, I spoke as a child, I thought as a child; but when I became a man, I put away childish things." People who still experience guilt when they blurt out an occasional swear word, lose their temper from time to time, forget to say grace before meals, enjoy a raunchy joke and the like are still apt to worry about how stepping on cracks may affect their mothers' backs.

Far more serious and far more fertile sources of contemporary guilt feelings reside in our acquired self-expectations, over-inflated sense of responsibility, ambition, and the notion that we must not only be perfect, but be all things to all people.

It all starts in childhood when we perceive and receive the hopes and expectations of parents and teachers (and others), many of them totally unrealistic, as to what we must do, become, live up to, if we are to please them and reach our maximum potential. We also make heroes and role models into icons whose fantastic prowess, wisdom, patience, and talents, we feel we must match. When we fail to do so—as fail we must—we begin to build a guilt complex which compounds itself over the years. We feed it fresh material every time we make a comparison in which we come out on the short end of the stick. We meet or read about people who seem to be accomplishing far more than we are, pulling things off with ease, having their cake and eating it too. We feel guilty and inadequate. We thrash around. We condemn ourselves for being lazy, for not trying harder, for wasting our time, for not saving money, for not, in short, being perfect in all the ways that it is possible to be perfect.

Guilt of this totally unrealistic sort permeates all stages of life except infancy and perhaps extreme old age. The slight boy who hates contact sports feels guilty for not being the football star he thinks his father wants him to be; the shy, plain daughter who is convinced that her mother would like to see her be the most popular girl in high school cannot ease her guilt no matter how many A's she garners through hard study. The mother who feels that she is totally out of sync with the times because "all" she is doing is staying home, taking care of the kids, and doing the cleaning feels guilt. But then perhaps so does the working mother who feels she must be neglecting the children in potentially harmful fashion because she carts them off to the day care center all week long.

Parental Guilt

Which brings us to what many experts believe to be the mother lode of contemporary guilt—the great parental national anthem: "Oh where did we go wrong?"

Otherwise intelligent, realistic women and men,

adults who know the score, who accept the odds of
Murphy's Law ("If something can go wrong, it will
go wrong") as it applies to almost every area of modern life and work, people who have long since learned
to roll with the punches, the setbacks, the breakdowns, the frustrations, the complexities and difficulties of trying to anticipate every possibility,
nonetheless expect themselves not only to be perfect
parents but to raise perfect children. When the children do not, in fact, turn out to be perfect, they inevitably and almost invariably blame themselves.

Given today's world, the ways in which children,
teen-agers, and young adults, can fall short of parental hopes and dreams is dazzling. Just as dazzling is
the parents' willingness to accept the total blame in-
discriminately. Religious parents who did everything
they could to foster the same sort of devotion in their
offspring will embrace heavy guilt feelings when those
same children not only rebel against, but absolutely
reject any sort of religious practice or affiliation.
Whether or not they have an occasional drink at home,
parents are quick to accuse themselves of dereliction
when a child drinks heavily and/or develops a drug
habit. Teen-age premarital sex and pregnancy is just
as rampant as is the guilt of the parents who in no
way promoted, abetted, or condoned such actions and
consequences.

Even though the traditional theory that homosex-
uality is the result of a domineering mother and a
weak, absent, or indifferent father has been virtually
discredited, parents, especially mothers, still wonder
just what it was they did to cause such a sexual orien-

tation in their son or daughter. Accusing oneself of creating a homosexual child is really terribly arrogant, since even psychiatrists and social anthropologists are divided as to whether the cause lies somewhere in biological factors or in environmental ones—nobody has been able to prove a definitive case for either.

And, if parental guilt can exist in the minds of happily married couples, it positively thrives among the divorced and separated. So much has been written about the horrendous effects of broken homes on children, one wonders, would the results have been different if a child was raised in a strained and hostile environment.

The great parental guilt trip rests squarely on the fact that, as Psychiatrist Emery Hetrick of New York University School of Medicine puts it, "parents take too much responsibility for their children." They are so emotionally involved that they totally forget that while their concern is intense, theirs is far from the only potent influence on the life of a modern child. They also forget that a child is a unique individual, not a carbon copy of either parent, nor even a sum of parental values, abilities, morality, likes and dislikes, hopes, or personality. It is this same emotional shortsightedness and intensity which makes parents (who are usually quick to forgive so much in their children) absolutely unforgiving to the point of mental sadism with themselves. They can neither forgive nor forget what they mistakenly imagine they have done to or failed to do for their children.

Parental guilt must be recognized for what it is and rooted out relentlessly. To help her millions of readers

do just that, columnist Ann Landers devoted an en-
tire column to the subject last year. It's a powerful ex-
change and I am happy to be able to share it with you
here by special permission.

* * *

DEAR ANN LANDERS:
   This letter is not in search of advice, nor am I looking for a shoulder to cry on. I've done enough cry-
ing. It's a message to parents of teenagers who have
rebelled against authority.
   I had two sons by my first husband. The oldest is 18
and out on the streets by choice. I say by choice because he chose not to conform to the rules of my home.
   At age 15 he chose to live with his father where
there was more money, more luxury and more freedom. At age 17 he chose to start stealing to support
a drug habit that he also chose to start. He was picked
up by the police after a witness saw him break into
a car to steal radio equipment. He was sent through
the juvenile court system where he also chose to break
the rules set down by the judge.
   The straw that broke the camel's back was when his
father came home during the day and found him and
his girfriend in bed while a nurse and the boy's invalid grandmother were downstairs watching TV.
   This kid chose to destroy two households, disregard
his religious upbringing and break the hearts of the
people who cared for him the most. He can't blame
it on a broken home because his father and I backed
each other to the hilt. We presented a united front even

though we were no longer married. Our personal feelings were set aside when it came to dealing with the boys. Their stepfather treated them as though they were his own. They were given love, guidance and discipline.

The point I want to make is this: You parents who are carrying a load of guilt because your kids went wrong should straighten up, stand tall and get on with your lives. These young people are this way because they chose to be. They will either hit bottom and climb back up, or they will hit bottom and stay there. It must be their choice. You cannot make the decision for them.

I still love my son deeply, and I'll be there if he decides to straighten up, but until that happens he's on his own.

TULSA PARENT

Ann Landers replies:

DEAR TULSA:

You've written a letter that is sure to strike a chord in the hearts of an enormous number of parents.

It is assumed by many that if a child is given love, firm guidelines and emotional support, he will turn out just fine. This is not always true. I have seen too many exceptions. I've also seen it work in reverse— children raised by alcoholic, violent, or permissive, uncaring parents with virtually no guidelines who turned out to be winners.

I don't pretend to know all the answers. For sure I

don't know the answer for this one. All we can do is our best. I have said it before and I will say it again: There comes a time when individuals must take responsibility for what they have become. Unfortunately, some children carry rebellion too far. They self-destruct in an effort to spit in the eye of authority and 'lead their own lives.'

I believe the proliferation of drugs in our society has a great deal to do with the ruination of millions of young people. Small wonder. Their sports heroes admit to using speed and cocaine and make a barrel of money in the bargain.

* * *

Filial Guilt

The flip side of parental guilt is also a pervasive modern source of stress. Powerful feelings of self-accusation trouble an increasing number of American adult "children" who believe that they have sinned against gratitude, affection and responsibility when they send their aging parent(s) off to a nursing home or other institution which provides professional care for the elderly and infirm. While such decisions have never been pleasant, they are being forced on more and more people today because so many Americans are living longer and longer.

The first step taken by many caring children is to try to make room for aging parents in their own homes and lives. Sometimes this works, at least when a parent is mobile and capable of basic self-sufficiency and

HOW I RELAX

I have different approaches for different types of stress. If a person is stressful, I try—if at all possible—to keep dealings with that person at a minimum (children exempted, of course). If an issue is the cause of the difficulty, I think it through *to death.* I imagine best and worst-case scenarios. And then I throw the whole mess in the lap of the gods. One small piece of philosophy which I find useful (and which may have come from *Fiddler on the Roof),* is the old Jewish saying: There are only two possibilities. It will either work out. . .or it won't.

I also have a high degree of acceptance, even for things that are not pleasing; if that's the way it is, that's the way it is. When things are absolutely *awful* I go to sleep, even in the daytime. This offers a new beginning and calamities seem less threatening. Things always seem more manageable by daylight, by the way, so the trick is to have stress confront you in daylight. Darkness did not get that name for nothing.

Margo Howard
Author and Critic

personal care. But in many more instances the effort
ultimately fails because it so radically disrupts the lifestyle of the host family. (Something which will be dis-
cussed in more detail in Chapter Three.)

Dealing with the problems presented by aging
parents is, as Harold S. Kushner (writing about the
ordeal of a man struggling to reach the right decision
in such a situation in *When Bad Things Happen to
Good People* (Avon, $3.95) says, "difficult under any
circumstances. The guilt feelings, the ambivalence
were there from the start. The helplessness of aging
parents, their appeals to their children tap feelings of
inadequacy, buried resentment, and guilt in many perfectly decent people. It is a hard situation to handle
under the best of conditions. The parents are often
scared, vulnerable, and sometimes emotionally im-
mature as well. They may not be above using illness,
loneliness, or guilt to manipulate their children into
giving them the attention they desperately need."

When, as is so often the case, the children realize
that for a host of practical reasons, the only workable
choice is to place parents in a care institution, they
begin to experience strong guilt feelings about abandoning their responsibility and betraying filial love.

In his book *Your Aging Parents* (Thomas More
Press, $7.95), John Deedy quotes Raymond Johnson
of Wartburg Lutheran Home for the Aged: "It's a common form of response, and not a particularly valid
one. . . . Many people feel that they are abandoning
their mother or their father when they place either or
both of them in a nursing home. It happens even
though it is very clear to them that they have done

everything possible and that their last choice for the loved one is having her or him admitted to a nursing home. But knowing the facts does not alleviate the feeling of guilt."

But it really should. Deedy points out that some nursing homes offer family counseling to help people understand their guilt, including group therapy sessions where people share the experience of others for support. "In this context," writes Deedy, "a Johnson rule of thumb is worth keeping in mind: Those who experience guilt are generally the ones without real guilt. Why? 'Because the person who feels guilt is the person who is concerned, a person who has tried to do all that could be done. It is often the person who does not feel guilt, who just doesn't give a darn, who should be the one carrying any burden of conscience.' "

Deedy also describes instances where adult children are made to feel what he calls "laid-on guilt," that inflicted by selfish, embittered "or otherwise malcontent aged parents." He cites the aged mother who complains about not being called or visited every day, or is constantly complaining that no one loves her anymore, and the father who makes the same sort of protests only in more indirect fashion. There are also stinging comments from friends and relatives who proclaim loudly that they would never allow their parents to be shut away in a nursing home.

Says Deedy: "Persons who allow themselves to feel guilt under the weight of such comments are very silly, for this is not guilt. The comments are unreasonable, or at the very least, unnecessary. As long as an individual is trying to do what he or she believes is decent and good, and best for the parent, that person should feel no guilt whatsoever.''

Finally, some older people can become so unreasonably demanding that they completely abuse the instinct of filial love and concern. Their children may never quite escape some feelings of guilt about minimizing their contacts with them, but it is impossible to try to please such irascible personalities. Of her perpetually discontented 88-year-old mother, a 60-year-old daughter who made many sacrifices and spent years caring for her at home writes:

"My mother has always been a complainer, and my father left her when I was graduated from high school at the age of 16. In those days divorce was a terrible thing (it still is) and my mother's ego was shattered. Foolishly, I spent the intervening years trying to make up to her for her disappointments and frustrations— until this past year. She was not satisfied living alone after her companion and friend became a nursing home resident. She was not satisfied living with us. She was not satisifed living in a nursing home where she opted to go after a severe arthritic attack. And she is still not satisfied in the adult congregate home where she now resides. Over the past two years she has become increasingly hostile to me, and six months ago the relationship completely fell apart. I simply have no more to give to this woman. My children stop by to see her occasionally, but the visit consists of a litany of her medical complaints and how badly I have treated her. For my sanity, my health, and my marriage, I have had to withdraw from this punishing relationship. Incidentally, I do still continue to look after the interests of my mother's now 94-year-old former companion—a unique and gracious lady."

Housecleaning—Be Your own Guilt-Buster

Bearing in mind that what you are aiming for is the elimination of irrational or undeserved guilt (not all guilty feelings, and especially not the faculty for experiencing guilt itself, which is an essential part of the human moral faculty), take a close look at those things about which you experience constant or recurring guilt and shame—the things that nag and accuse, that haunt and bring on bouts of self-reproach.

Look at them one by one. Too often, because they are painful feelings, people tend to lump all their guilt feelings into a sort of amorphous glob in which one thing blends into and overlaps another. A man's realization that he spends far too much time away from home, whether because he thinks his job demands it or simply because he is selfishly setting aside time for golf, bowling or other things he enjoys, may translate into guilt feelings about neglecting or not really loving his wife and children, of putting his marriage itself in jeopardy. His wife's reproachful looks may provoke all these feelings as a confusing, painful jumble. This in turn may cause him to stay away from home and her even more frequently, because it's easier to evade the proximate source of his guilt than it is to sort it out, understand it, and take the steps needed to change his behavior so he no longer has to feel guilty.

In his case he should feel the guilt appropriate to his

obligations as a husband and father. But it is a stress
that can be removed only by changing his lifestyle.
As we have seen, however, there are other instances in
which a cold, objective look at personal guilt will reveal its source and cause to be grounded in false expectations which have been imposed on us by others
or by ourselves. The mother who wrote to Ann Landers about her son, the woman who wrote about her
mother, both made such an appraisal of their own
stress and decided to absolve themselves of any guilt
feelings. They came to the objective realization that
they were under no obligation to take the responsibility for what other people chose to do or become, even
though they loved and cared for them.

To get rid of this sort of unnecessary guilt it is essential to isolate it, to separate it from the glob, and exam-
ine it almost formally—put it on trial, just as it has
put you on trial. Go back to its beginnings—on what
grounds did it take its initial root in your conscience?
Have those grounds since been proven false by your
own subsequent experience and knowledge? Are you
reproaching yourself for something you think you did
or didn't do which in reality would have had no bearing on the outcome? (Many of us are haunted by "If
onlys...." If only I hadn't left the house that day
Mother wouldn't have had her stroke. If only I had
taken the Interstate we wouldn't have had the wreck
which killed Mary and Tom.... None of which have
any basis in reality.)

Another kind of guilt that is a likely candidate for
the dust bin is guilt by false association and assump-
tion. Children may be the most easily victimized by

this tandem, but so are many adults and in both cases the guilt evoked hangs on forever, even when its victims should have long outgrown it. This is the sort of guilt one feels when a divorce takes place and a child feels that she or he must somehow be to blame, or was not sufficiently lovable. This is what goes down when we lose our tempers, say or think hateful things about someone and then, when something terrible does in fact, but by sheer coincidence, happen to them, we feel directly responsible.

Then there is the guilt that afflicts those who are overtaken by misfortunes of fate or circumstances. The classic examples of this are the mother who runs to answer the phone and returns to find her child drowned or scalded in the bathtub; the motorist who runs over an old person who suddenly walks out from behind a parked car; the father who forgot to have the furnace serviced whose family burns to death in the house fire that breaks out while he is on a business trip. Unlike "if only" guilt there is real evidence that what was done or not done makes a tragic difference, but the subsequent guilt is really not justified because there was abolutely no malice intended or involved. The most these people should reproach themselves with is carelessness of the sort that we all exhibit on a fairly regular basis and perhaps not even that. But because the results were so much more serious than the inconvenience of forgetting one's car keys, or neglecting to pay the electric bill, they charge themselves with murder. For such individuals, and those who get caught up in the myriad variations on the scenario which modern life can serve up, it will be difficult to cut this heavy but grossly disproportionate guilt down to size without some professional counseling. They should seek it out because their lives can be rendered miserable until they do.

Finally, there are some things that we did or didn't do which, though highly regrettable, are also irreversible—done and over with. Denying that we are guilty of them is impossible, but having clearly shouldered our blame and resolving not to make the same mistake again, there is little to be gained by continuing to use guilt as a means of punishing ourselves. It is not easy to manage this but it can be done if you will gather up such feelings and put them in a mental compartment marked "Regrets."

When the incident pushes itself forward, demanding a fresh bout of stressful guilt feelings, remind yourself that you've been over this often enough, and that all the appropriate guilt is now stored away under Regrets. Anytime you want to take it out and relive it, the incident and all its guilt associations are there, ready and waiting. But now is not the time. A little shame may overflow and give you a twinge, but if dealt with promptly in this abstract but formalized mental discipline, your "Regrets" file will prove invaluable.

Self-Forgiveness

Being forgiven is one of the sweetest of reliefs. As children we all can remember the moments when the cloud of parental disapproval would suddenly be lifted and we came back into the sunshine of tempor-

HOW I RELAX

I gave up stress for Lent in 1967—and never got back to it. Honest!

Erma Bombeck
Author, Columnist, Humorist

arily rescinded affection. Whether unilateral or mutual, the "making up" moment between lovers is a bliss that challenges love-making itself. If only human beings can experience shame and guilt, then only humans can know the wonder of reconciliation and forgiveness.

The time-worn adage that "to err is human but to forgive is divine," doesn't mean that only God can forgive. It means that we are most like God, or at least at our human best, when we extend the mercy of forgiveness. And we do forgive each other, even when we fail to forget what the transgression was. The trouble is that too many who are ready, willing and generous in their forgiveness of others, are virtually incapable of either forgiving or forgetting their own lapses or of absolving themselves from the attendant guilt.

The art of self-forgiving has been rendered very suspect by a culture which has too closely associated it with the ignominy of making self-excuses, of trying to put personal blame on others ("It was Eve that made me eat the apple," protested the craven Adam.) We know ourselves too well, we suspect our own motives, we know our capacity for justifying our own selfishness, laziness and craving for instant gratification. How could such a person ever deserve forgiveness?

The answer is that nobody "deserves" forgiveness; it is a gift of compassion and a recognition of human weakness which says, "Okay, you behaved like a rat, a spoiled child, a pompous, uncaring ass—but that doesn't mean you are totally worthless; I still love you." Christ's precept that his followers "love your neighbor as yourself" has its echoes in all faiths. If we are to care about what happens to other people we must also care about ourselves. If we love them simply for who they are, then we must first love ourselves for what we are—warts and all. If we are able to bring ourselves to forgive others, we must also be able to forgive ourselves.

When guilt has you tied up in knots, when you feel the most shame and the least sense of personal worth and esteem, when you feel you are the least deserving and least lovable person alive, try a little self-forgiveness. It doesn't matter that you don't deserve it, you have forgiven others, why not yourself?

As we will see in the next two chapters, there is more than enough heavy, often inescapable stress in the world without carrying the additional back-breaking load of needless guilt.

CHAPTER TWO
Our Stress-Filled World

An Anxious Age

AMERICANS in the 80s are "people who worry about weight on Monday and nuclear winter on Tuesday," says author Ellen Goodman. We've got so many things to worry about today, thanks to our brave new electronic, laser beam, multi-mediafied world, that we worry about being complacent during those rare moments when we forget to worry about anything else.

People have more or less always been anxious about such inevitabilities as death and taxes and about such chronic problems as war, unemployment, illness, poverty and domestic problems. And the stress experienced by those of generations past who actually were overtaken or caught up by one or more of these situations was certainly real. But for the majority at least, there were long stretches of not exactly tranquility, but periods when life seemed to roll along without constant tension. There were always annoyances, of course, and things may have been a bit dull. But dullness is at least one version of peace of mind.

This is a highly simplified and complacent vision, of course. There have been great wars, famines, earthquakes, plagues, murders, revolutions, and near genocides all through human history which have been disastrous experiences for countless thousands. The thing is, however, that until relatively recently, unless you were there, in it, you probably didn't care, for the

simple reason that you didn't know it was going on—
or at least not until it was over.

The Indians of the American plains had problems of
their own in the 18th century but they did not compound them with worries about the Reign of Terror in
Paris. They didn't feel anxiety, as well they might
have, about the combination of economic, political
and demographic factors that were conspiring to send
a wave of settlers and soldiers into their land and
which would destroy their very way of life in the 19th
century.

What has happened since, especially in the last two-
thirds of this century, is that we have become what
Marshall McLuhan termed a "Global Village." We are
all linked to each other by communications; we are,
for better or worse, almost instantly made aware of
most of the trouble in the world—most of the threats,
the trends, the probabilities and the consequences.
The result is a whole new dimension of worry and
anxiety.

The Acceleration of Change

At the same time, as Alvin Toffler has so effectively
shown in his 1970 best-seller, *Future Shock*, the rate
of change in virtually every aspect of life—science,
technology, economics, medicine, communications
—has accelerated so rapidly that it threatens to outstrip our innate human capacity to adapt to the new.
Traditional perceptions of social stability, inter-per-
sonal relations, religious and moral traditions, work
and play, travel, have all, to varying degrees, been
thrown up for grabs.

"We may define future shock," Toffler writes, "as the distress, both physical and psychological, that arises from an overload of the human organism's physical adaptive system and its decision-making processes. Put more simply, future shock is the human response to over-stimulation."

He quotes British novelist and scientist C.P. Snow who said that "until this century," social change was "so slow that it would pass unnoticed in one person's lifetime. That is no longer so. The rate of change has increased so much that our imagination can't keep up." As social psychologist Warren Bennis puts it: "No exaggeration, no hyperbole, no outrage can realistically describe the extent and pace of change. In fact, only the exaggerations appear to be true."

Simply trying to keep up with changes in our world is a major backdrop for the activation of stressful factors. It is something like the extraordinary amount of alertness which tourists experience when they are suddenly faced with the strange new settings, people, customs, language, and currency of a foreign land. It is exhilarating, but it is also very exhausting— especially if the vacation is lengthy and covers many different countries. As the cliche has it, there are any number of "nice places to visit," but one wouldn't want to live there. The relief of getting home is very real. We can "turn ourselves off" and settle back into familiar routines and customs.

But what if, as the plots of more than a few science fiction novels and futuristic movies have asked us to imagine, home has changed while we were off traveling? Changed so much that it now seems as strange and challenging as the foreign lands just visited? Such a science fiction scenario would cause a storm of stress in real life because there would then be no "normal" or familiar routine to settle back into; a new and strange world must be absorbed and a whole new set of adaptive procedures learned.

When persons move to a new home (as one in four Americans do each year), especially to a different town or part of the country, something like this happens. It is stressful, but because our customs nationally are now so homogenized, and family ties, though stretched, are not severed, it is usually manageable in itself. But one needn't be uprooted to experience the stress of change in dozens of areas of contemporary life. In effect, for anyone over fifty, the world into which she or he was born has changed almost as radically as if they had moved to a foreign country of the future. It didn't happen all at once, but as Toffler and others have pointed out, it has happened at a rate alarmingly faster than in the past. And, even though human beings are the most adaptable of all creatures, being blessed with a brain that has absorbed, invented, coped and imagined its way not only to survival but to mastery of the world and now stands pointed to take on space, as well, we may have our limits in terms of how much change, and the accompanying stress it inevitably generates, we can handle.

Generic Anxiety

Because we live one day at a time, and are usually preoccupied with the immediate goals and troubles

HOW I RELAX

I really don't have any "tricks" or "rituals" which relieve me of stress. But there are certain situations in which I find that stress is lessened and I try to "create" these situations when I feel the need to relax.

I find that relaxing at home alone helps. I like to go home, turn off the telephone, dress in some comfortable clothes and spend an evening doing what I want to do rather than what someone else wants. I may read, listen to music, do some things I have neglected to do for some time (such as weeding out books in my library, straightening out my personal files or desk drawers) or, in good weather, take a walk.

Another relaxing experience is to have a leisurely meal with friends, either at my home or theirs, or even at a favorite restaurant.

Finally, my quiet hour of prayer early each morning before the rest of the house is up is essential to my well-being. Without that hour or "centering," I'd find it difficult to cope with the rest of the day."

Cardinal Joseph Bernardin
Archbishop of Chicago

thereof, it's relatively easy to forget temporarily many of the things that are lurking, just beyond our conscious mind, to emerge and demand their share of attention and anxiety. These form what might be called "generic" worries that inhabit the modern, reasonably well-informed American adult mind. They are always there waiting for a situation or an event to summon them into the foreground where they can add their jolt of stress. Not all of them are new, of course, but that doesn't make them less potent.

Many of them are new, however, and more of these stack up every month in our slam-bang world. Consider air travel, for example. Let's suppose that I have finally managed, perhaps with the help of such potentially destructive coping devices as two martinis and a couple of tranquilizers, to handle my innate fear of entrusting my land-bound body to the mysterious mechanical mercies of a huge metal monster that hurls me through the air at a speed and at a height which violate my every physically evolved instinct. Suppose I even manage to deal with the announcement that abominable weather conditions prevail at the airport of my destination—runways covered by the same glaze of ice which may be even now building up on the wings of the plane and quite likely sealing the landing gear inside its housing.

Suppose further that if and when the plane lands safely, I must rush to a business appointment which is crucial to my career and the outcome of which depends on how well I make a long and complicated presentation.

All of these anxieties were already stored in my head

before take-off. The trip itself has released them and they are causing a great deal of stress. I find myself in a situation from which I want to escape. There is no escape, of course. But that easily grasped fact does not turn off the pounding of my heart or the tension that has me in its grip. I am consoled and kept in control by two other factors, however: I anticipated much of this stress, and I have a sound, rational conviction that it will soon end. I am also kept in control by the presence and behavior of my fellow passengers.

If they are all sitting there so calmly, reading magazines, sipping coffee, engaging in small talk, they must not be feeling the anxiety I am experiencing. Therefore, while my stress is very real to me, its causes must rest solely in my imagination. I will not make a fool of myself by letting my anxiety show beyond keeping a tight grip on the arm of the seat and sweating a little. (If God had wanted me to fly he would have given me guts.)

But now suppose the unexpected, the totally unanticipated happens: two men wearing ski masks emerge from the lavatory at the rear of the plane brandishing hand grenades. My stress becomes overwhelming and turns into panic. And at the same time the reassuring behavior of fellow passengers breaks down completely. Suddenly the screw of stress has been turned too tightly. Now there is no reason to believe that the trip will soon be over or that it will have a safe landing. Everyone's whole nervous system is sending out powerful signals that it's time to fight or escape. Reason is blanked out. Anything can happen and may: a passenger may attack the hi-jackers; some will scream,

others will vomit, faint, or have heart attacks. Ah! The
joys of modern air travel.

To the generic anxiety about flying which I—and
thousands of others—carry around with me, I, all my
fellow passengers, and all those who see reports of our
misadventure can now add another file: the possibility of being hi-jacked.

Everywhere You Turn

Anxiety is the holding pattern for stress. It is in itself
a form of low-level stress. As noted, what probably
saves us is that it is virtually impossible to worry about
all the things there are to worry about at any one time.
Current concerns preoccupy our minds but there, in
the background, is everything else. And today that
everything else is broader in scope than at any time in
history because of our global consciousness and because we live in the age of instant information.

To make a list of all the things that are capable of
exerting stress on we pioneers of the computer age
is virtually impossible. But even a brief survey may
be useful to those who sometimes wonder why, even
when things are going relatively well, when one is in
good health, has a roof over one's head, food in the
kitchen, a steady job and enough money to pay the
month's bills, one can still feel ill-at-ease, apprehen-
sive, worn-out, and surrounded by what novelist
Walker Percy has coined as "free-floating motes of
anxiety." It is not some personal neurosis, it is not
an inability to manage, it is not a failure of character.
It is simply that all too many of us are operating dan-

gerously near overload. We have too much; we try to do too much; and most of all, we know too much. This is complicated by living in a world that offers too many options, too many products, too many novelties (some 1,500 new patents are applied for each day around the world) and which has conditioned all of us to expect instant answers and solutions to problems—problems many of which either require long-term human cooperation and revolutionary dedication, or which may have no satisfactory solution. This does not mean that these massive difficulties are not real—the 1985 *Britannica Book of the Year* features lengthy articles on "Our Disintegrating World: The Menace of Global Anxiety," and "Nuclear Winter: Its Discovery and Implications"—but they will not yield to any individual action on the part of those who worry about them.

Examples of the latter are such pervasive concerns as:

- the arms race and nuclear holocaust
- world-wide terrorism
- over-population
- abortion versus right-to-life
- social justice and economic parity for the Third World
- the African famine
- racism
- crime
- ecological problems ranging from acid rain to the ravages of the "greenhouse" effect.

On a more immediate and personal level. We worry
about:

- cancer in all its malignant varieties
- heart attacks and strokes
- eating the right foods
- being overweight
- getting sufficient exercise
- contracting herpes or AIDS
- Alzheimer's Disease
- high blood pressure
- cholesteral
- smoking and its effect on non-smokers
- alcohol and drug abuse.

We harbor deep-seated concerns about our husbands, wives, lovers, children, parents and relatives,
and our relationships with them:

Are we still in love or are we simply staying together out of habit and convenience?

Am I failing my aging parents?

Am I making unconscious but potentially destructive decisions and rules for my children?

Is it safe to let the kids walk to and from school
alone these days?

As a working mother, am I really doing justice to
the children?

What kind of influences, experiences and diseases are they being exposed to at the Day Care Center?

Where did I/we go wrong in producing this rebellious, freakish, surly teen-ager?

Donna is so withdrawn—is suicide really a possibility for young people with their whole lives ahead of them?

Am I really expected to advise a teen-aged girl about the use of contraceptives?

How can I get the kids to go to church/temple?

Divorce is rampant among my friends—will we be next?

Is marriage itself in trouble?

What should I do about my daughter and her "friend" living together?

Why hasn't Timmy had a date with a girl all through high school?

We worry about our neighborhoods, our houses and condominiums and rising rent and real-estate taxes. We fret about the gouging interest rates compounding on our outstanding credit card balances; about car payments and repair bills; about our myriad appliances that are constantly going on the blink. The approach

of April 15th puts thousands of people into a prolonged income tax trauma which often fails to sub-
side even after all the fiendishly complicated forms
have been submitted on time. (How do you spell indigestion? AUDIT)

What Will the Neighbors Think?

Worry about our precious self-image is as pervasive
as the common cold, and twice as stressful. It begins
in the teen years and builds. Parents worry not only
about their own image in the community, but about
everything their children do and say, as well. How
many nights of tossing and turning have been wasted
trying to figure out how to put the best possible face
on a family problem that concerns no one else? Modern life is stressful enough without fruitless worry over
what the neighbors will say, what mother or Aunt
Ethel will think, or how to explain it to the gang at
work.

Obsessive concern with the opinions of others is
pointless. As Eleanor Roosevelt so wisely observed:
"We wouldn't worry so much about what other people think, if we knew how little they did."

Give Us This Day Our Daily Stress

Mental anxiety is not the only form of low-level
stress. Our daily routine is another rich source. The
commuter finds plenty of it on the way to work. Traffic jams and road conditions produce tensions in those
who drive. Long waits for buses and trains, snow,

rain, frost and heat, jostling crowds and constant noise are the alternative.

Certain jobs are definitely more stressful than others —surgeons, air traffic controllers, teachers in inner-city schools, para-medics and many others work under constant stress. But it's not relaxing to be a mother trying to cope with a houseful (often one or two are enough) of small children, or a cab driver fighting gridlock, or an overburdened, underpaid secretary, either. Every occupation has its stresses, including the highly underrated stress of monotony.

All of us meet deadlines every day. Getting to work on time; keeping the work flowing; seeing to the myriad of chores of living, from shopping to housework; getting the kids dressed and off to school; remembering birthdays and anniversaries; keeping ourselves bright and alert in the presence of those we work with; biting our tongues for the sake of tact; expressing concern and interest when we actually have none; somehow managing to get through the whole bloody routine for the ten thousandth time; curbing our temper; suffering fools gladly; adding yet another responsibility to our already endless list—all these things and more add their straw to the pile that threatens to break our back. There are days when we all understand the truth of the adage that "just getting out of bed in the morning is an heroic act."

CHAPTER THREE
Stress for All Seasons

IN keeping with the growing complexity of our nuclear age, there are special stresses for each phase of life. Again, many of these are as old as humankind itself, while others arrive virtually daily on the scene. Until recently who worried about AIDS, joggers knee, or employee eye strain from long hours of work on Video Display Terminals?

Childhood and Adolescence

Infancy and childhood are celebrated in all our minds as the carefree years. And all things being relative, that is true. There are, in fact, quite a number of childhood stresses—frustrations, fears, going to school, learning to compete, not to mention the primal stress of being expelled from the tranquility of the womb at birth itself. There can be special stresses in the lives of young children whose parents get divorced, just as there are some traumatic stresses in the lives of millions of children who are forced to live with poverty, hunger and disease.

It is not to make light of any of these anxieties, stresses and deprivations to say that they are tempered by, even if not dispelled, by the marvelous resilience of childhood, and aside from the grinding stresses of poverty, they pale when weighed against those to come. By comparison, adolescence is a time so fraught with stress for both the teen-ager and parent that there are some days when it seems like it really ought to be cancelled altogether.

From the teen-ager's point of view almost everything is suddenly up for grabs. The world of home,
brothers and sisters and neighborhood playmates retreats behind a blinding new self-consciousness which
exerts an almost unbearable stress. The peer group
now becomes all-important. It must see the teen-ager
as she or he desperately needs to be seen—as accept-
able, as pretty, as rugged, as cool, as funny, as prop-
erly dressed, as independent, as sexy, as athletic, etc.
Failure to measure up in any area brings instant tor-
ment. And, since nobody outside the movies and vid-
eos can possibly be perfection, a state of inner misery
and turmoil usually exists around the clock. Some will
cope with it better than others who will try to ease
the pain with drugs and boozo. Some will go even further and flirt with or actually attempt the ultimate
attention-getter—suicide. Most will struggle on
through, living from day to day, alternating between
jubilant elation and terrible downers.

It's all part of the broad pattern of physical and emotional stress and ambivalence which adolescents experience. I have never seen it better summed up than
by Dr. Theodore Lidz, professor of psychiatry at Yale
University. Adolescence, he says, "is a time of seeking: a seeking inward to find who one is; a searching
outward to locate one's place in life; a longing for
another with whom to satisfy cravings for intimacy
and fulfillment. It is a time of turbulent awakening
to love and beauty, but also of days darkened by loneliness and despair. It is a time of carefree wandering
of the spirit through realms of fantasy and in pursuit
of idealistic visions, but also of disillusionment and

disgust with the world and self. It can be a time of adventure with wonderful episodes of reckless folly but also of shame and regret that linger. Adolescents live with a vibrant sensitivity that carries them to ecstatic heights and lowers them to almost untenable depths."

Young Adults

Young adults, whether upwardly mobile or not, can celebrate about one thing—they are finally done with the terrible teens. But they have hardly had time to say goodbye to their last zit before it's time to face the awesome prospect of taking up life on their own and living up to all those great expectations which their parents have for them, and which they have for themselves. Freedom can be an awesome thing.

Young women and men who go to college, which presents its own arsenal of competitive stresses, especially for those who have opted for one of the professions, may postpone shaking hands with self-sufficiency for a while, but it is still out there waiting for them—the prospect of having nobody but oneself to fall back on. Career choices can be agonizing. Failure to get into the field of one's choice can be demoralizing. Many have to face up to the fact that dreams may have to yield to the hard realities of both the job market and a ruthless professional assessment of how much talent they really have. It can mean settling for less—a lot less. This is the time when young people who have always said that they would be writers, actresses, doctors, lawyers or ballet stars may

have to bite the bullet and accept certain limitations
and the prospect of more ordinary and routine voca-
tions and careers.

A first job presents stresses that are as unique as they
are unrelenting. To be constantly under the gun of a
critical boss, to work with people you haven't chosen
as friends day after day is a strain. So is keeping your
emotions in tight rein. At work, emotional outbursts
are not smiled upon. Forced conformity in dress
codes, hours, body language and cheerfulness are an
eight-hour strain; so is being confined to a desk or office; so is the unrelenting expectation of punctuality.
So is commuting, rushing around all day Saturday to
do the domestic chores, banking and shopping that
will get you through the next week.

And wonder of wonders, there are people around
who resent you, who are competing with you on an
all-out basis. Not just the competition of sports which
is soon over and done with, not the competition of the
classroom which is settled by a teacher. No, this is
all out war for a promotion that can make a very real
and lasting difference in your life. And it's all going
on behind a smokescreen of smiles and memos. To
the young adult it may well seem like a bad dream.
Tension anyone?

As a result of the Women's Liberation Movement, as
well as other social factors, many young women find
themselves under a stressor that their mothers—at
least the majority of their mothers—did not have to
deal with. A young woman, in her late twenties, married, with a Masters in Business Administration and
a job with a prestigious electronics firm in California,

HOW I RELAX

For me, the greatest stress in being a fire fighter is the uncertainty. I never do more than catnap on duty because I don't want to have to respond to an alarm from a dead sleep. I put worry from my mind by being as completely prepared physically and mentally as possible. Skating and running take care of the first, and imaging helps with the second.

Before a race, I go through it completely in my imagination, seeing the course, the competition, and myself every meter of the way. Responding to a fire alarm I run a "worst-possible-case" scenario in my head. Then I put it all away and get on with it.

Over the years I've taught myself not to try to be a perfectionist or a fanatic about any one part of my life. In the beginning, all my ego was on the starting line of every race. Once you've won your share it doesn't seem as crucial, because you can't win them all. I also came to realize that you can't make everybody happy and you can't control some things. After you've prepared and planned and done your best nothing is gained by stewing over what can or has gone wrong.

When I get too many things on my schedule I find it helps to make a list and stick in your pocket—otherwise your mind keeps rehashing what you have to do.

Besides a daily break, I've discovered that a really different sort of vacation makes for complete relaxation—one that gets you totally away from the usual people and scene.

Jack Mortell
Fire Fighter and Two-time National
Indoor Speedskating Champion

says, "I feel that I (and many others like me) experience a lot of pressure to make a choice between family and career—and, unfortunately, I think the family is losing out to career. This may be more the result of our perception that a career is what is expected from a modern woman than from a genuine desire for a career for its own sake. There is a sizable group that fool themselves too long about what it is they really want out of life. Having gotten an education and perhaps advanced degrees and working for a few years, they suddenly find themselves fast approaching 30 and realizing that as far as marriage and family go, it's now or never. Then there's a search for a husband that often requires a lot of stress and perhaps compromise. Personal desires and fulfillment are also complicated by financial demands. These days it almost always takes two incomes to be able to afford a house, so even after we marry it may not be possible to start a family. I think there should be more emphasis in the late teens on preparing yourself to realize what it really is you want out of life. I feel I just recently stopped dwelling on every detail of the future. I was so focused on the proper timing to get everything in that I "wanted" or "should" do. In my case I believe my stress was from self-imposed expectations. But, of course, many of those self-expectations must rise out of what I think society expects of me."

Yuppies

Believe it or not, all is not well with even among the much-discussed, much-envied baby boomers who are devoting all their energies to becoming successful professionals. In the *Chicago Tribune* Clarence Page reports on the research of psychologist Douglas LaBier, a senior fellow at Washington, D.C.'s Project on Technology, Work and Character. He specialized in the problems of executive stress and has found convincing evidence that the "good life" of today's young, upwardly mobile professionals is exacting a heavy emotional and psychological toll. "The syndrome," he says, "covers a wide range of nagging emotional disorders, sometimes crossing the border from a general malaise to psychosomatic maladies, drug problems and even suicide."

One group of executives, prototypical Yuppies, 25 to 45 years old, he found to be "very sick though very well adjusted. They had molded themselves into the attitudes and values needed for success, but they also bottle up a lot of rage." Their complaints ran to a common theme of "compromises, trade-offs, anger and self-betrayal."

Dr. LaBier counsels them to analyze their values to find out if they are simply driving themselves for success' sake and to buy an endless stream of gadgets and luxuries they really don't need.

Comments *Tribune* columnist Page, "Behind the fancy psychobabble, it all boils down to a simple message: Man cannot live by bread alone, even when it is served with white wine and imported cheese."

Middle Age: The Crunch Generation

From Yuppies to Grumpies (Grown Up Mature People) is not a giant step but it is one that is inevitable. Just when middle age begins is debatable and largely irrelevant. For many men, as well as women, it is entered only after a personal wrestling with reality called the mid-life crisis. It's more than just accepting the fact that you are no longer young, but involves all sorts of other unsettling truths that have somehow been hiding themselves in the busy routine of making a living, raising a family, and generally being too preoccupied to sit down and sort things out.

You are not going to achieve fame and immortality; you have gone about as far as you are going to go in your job; you have a limited amount of time left to live; you tire out more easily, you don't like surprises as much as you once did, even though you are often bored; you have spent a lot of time and energy working and caring for others, so isn't it about time you did something for yourself? Maybe a new career is the answer. Maybe a new wife or lover will perk you up—that is if you can find one at your age. And so it goes, in some version or another.

It's a stressful time and it leads many people to do some very silly things they regret almost instantly. They also do some things in an effort to change their image—clothes, hair, lifestyle—that make them look ridiculous.

But, in many serious ways, middle age is what life is all about. John F. Kennedy once wrote something to the effect that it is upon the shoulders of mature people in their forties, fifties and sixties that the job of running the world descends. Not only are they the ones in positions of responsibility and power, but they have, or should have, garnered enough wisdom and vision to express the best that is in our civilization. They are charged with caring for and giving direction to the young and impetuous, while at the same time providing for the care and health of the old.

And indeed, this is exactly where many middle-aged Americans find themselves today, caught in a crunch between generations which have lately been extending themselves considerably and causing an increase in their respective overlapping demands.

As more and more young people opt for continuing education, defer marriage, and have difficulty in finding employment capable of making them independent, middle-aged parents find themselves having to continue both financial and emotional support for children who would have been long gone in the past. Some remain living with their parents while an ever-increasing number, having tried life on their own, come back home to live.

No matter how congenial this continuing close relationship with children who are no longer children may be (and it is often far from congenial; more like a strained truce), their presence can cause considerable stress and frustration. Stress, because parents have a hard time not exercising parental authority and concern as they have always done. It's hard to bite your tongue simply because a son or daughter is now 25 or 30. But you really don't want them bringing in friends and partying; you really would like to have the bathroom to yourself after all these years; you are tired to death of cooking large meals, hauling in groceries, doing laundry, answering the phone and taking messages. You feel frustration because you really do deserve some peace and quiet, not to mention a chance to spend your free time doing things you've always wanted to do. Being a "hands on" parent was not meant to be a lifetime job.

At the same time, the crunch can and often does come down from the other end of the scale—middle-aged parents must increasingly be prepared to take a varying amount of responsibility in caring for their own parents. This in itself is not new. What is new is the frequency and duration of the instances when such care is required.

Why? Because in this century, particularly since the end of World War II, Americans are living longer. At the turn of the century only four percent of the population were still around at age 65. Today that figure is almost 12 percent—25.5 million people 65 and older. The average American's life expectancy is approaching 75 years.

And that's good news, to be sure. But most of those 25.5 million people who are 65 and over are parents, and many of them are sooner or later going to require some help, some care, some substantial amount of time and concern and attention from their children. And these children, themselves no longer young, are the members of the Crunch Generation.

Once again, no matter how much love is involved, however generously the "child" responds to the needs of his or her parents, the problems involved in caring for the elderly can be as formidable as they are stressful. If an aging parent moves in with you, the reverse side of the returning child dilemma presents

HOW I RELAX

I find that remembering something nice said to or about me is soothing.

I find that keeping a diary—not necessarily every day or very seriously, is useful. On days when things seem rotten I can look back at whatever year is handy (the things aren't kept in any sort of order and a lot of them have crept out of sight and reach) and check a date same as the depressing one I'm having from out of the past. If I enjoyed that day I can say, "See, everything isn't always awful," and if the day then was a mess, too, I can say, "Okay, you survived that one, you'll survive this one, too."

As for getting to sleep (I often find it harder to stay awake), I find that not thinking about anything real, rather, say, about riding out west in a covered wagon, or being the mayor of a small seaside town, or entertaining in an arctic igloo (things should have lots of details involved) can bring on sleep.

And making oneself smile when things don't look good—even a dumb, clown-like smile, helps.

Joan Kahn
Mystery Editor
St. Martin's Press, New York

itself. No matter how well things appear to be going, you are having to make more space in your life, draw on reserves of care, energy, patience—not to mention the increased domestic work and the lack of privacy— than you really, down deep in that selfish spot in all of us, want to. And, when you throw in factors of ill-health, chronic problems of old age, and the fact that many aging parents still expect you to obey them in everything, it can cause the emotional blood-pressure to soar.

John Deedy sums it up neatly in his book *Your Aging Parents:* "Conflicts between parents and their children are as old as Genesis. They can also be chronic. They can ease or even seem to disappear, when the children go off on their own to start their own families, only to rekindle themselves in old age, when alteration of the dependency equation brings the once contentious family members back in close contact one with the other."

Additional stress can easily rise out of the simple fact that the aging parent is the aging parent of only one member of a Crunch Generation couple. If your husband never got along with his mother-in-law at a distance, he certainly isn't going to relate to her on an around-the-clock basis. And all this is compounded by another simple fact—a couple has four parents. There's no law that says that they will not all require care at the same time.

There are many scenarios, of course—putting aging parents into nearby apartments, retirement communities, nursing homes—but, as was noted in Chapter One, these alternatives can also produce stress and guilt.

Retirement and Old Age

Everybody knows that retirement is what the game is all about. It is the rainbow at the end of the rat race where we've stored our pot of golden IRAs, pension plans and Social Security benefits. Just think of it— not having to go to work, not just for a few weeks, but *ever*. Time to travel and garden and weave and make wonderful artifacts in the basement workshop; time to visit the kids and the grandchildren without having to rush between airports; time to read all those really worthwhile books that we never got around to; time to catch the big ones out at the lake; time for eighteen holes in the middle of the week when the golf course isn't teeming with duffers.

Sounds marvelous, doesn't it? Especially if you're a man. Maybe not so hot if you're his wife and don't care for golfing and fishing and maybe not even having a husband with nothing but time on his hands hanging around the house and kitchen all day; especially a husband who's used to being treated like a big shot at work where everybody is expected to agree with all his half-baked opinions and defer to his every command and wish. Is he going to expect three hot meals every day? If so then you are facing the prospect of less free time than ever. Is he going to change a lifetime habit of watching TV every evening and suddenly turn into Fred Astaire and go out on the town, take you to the theater and the symphony and to glorious adventures in gracious dining? No, he's already talking about how we have to make our retirement dollars stretch because inflation will be eating us up on our fixed income.

HOW I RELAX

What seems to be the highest stress situation occurs when I work on unfamiliar locations. I am in a factory; I know no one there until the moment I enter. It is absolutely necessary that I obtain an outstanding photograph by the end of the day. I might already be exhausted from travel. Scanning the scene reveals no sign of a view that is beautiful or exciting. The plant manager, the foreman and perhaps my client are watching me. They have not seen anything special, either. They are waiting to see what I can possibly come up with.

The solution to this stress: 1) There is definitely an outpouring or inpouring of something inside of me—adrenaline, I guess. 2) There is a great narrowing of focus. Sometimes it is an almost trance-like state. My terrific stress then immediately relieves itself in a direct line of action, like a bullet from a gun, but perhaps only mentally at first. I think that jobs like mine, which may appear to be impossibly stressful to an outsider, are actually possible to handle without undo stress because the stress (the burning gunpowder) is immediately relieved in a focused force (the bullet).

The most difficult part of the speeding bullet method of stress relief is how to stop a speeding bullet at five P.M. A couple of double martinis usually slow its trajectory sharply, but most of us are familiar with the hazards of that approach. A sauna followed by a swim and good session of lovemaking would be the perfectly civilized way to arrest the bullet's trajectory, but this solution never seems to be available.

Fortunately for me, my job usually entails a lot of physical effort—another great stress reliever. Between assignments, when I am working at home, I have great difficulty relieving stress because there is no speeding bullet effect, only a series of irritating confinements and blockages, similar, I suspect, to those experienced by people in typical office environments. There is no physical, muscular output of energy and, since my schedule is so erratic, I never get a regular exercise program established. When I do manage to exercise, though, it is a fantastic relaxer.

Tony Kelly
Freelance Photographer
Evanston, IL

And the man himself may discover that all that free
time soon begins to hang rather heavily around his
neck. After a bit he begins to realize not only that,
though he has the time for all the golfing and fishing
he dreamed of, he doesn't necessarily have the energy
for it, but also that he's suddenly not as sure of his
own self-importance and worth as he used to be. His
identity was somehow tied up with what he did, not
who he is. He doesn't get the respect he once took for
granted when he told people his title.

So, just when retirees think they've got it made and
have finally freed themselves from the stresses of the
daily grind, things like this pop up to add stresses
they've never imagined or encountered.

Stress is remarkably creative and possessed of
equally remarkable staying power. Aging people are
seldom free of it. Failing eyesight and hearing are perhaps inevitable, but that doesn't make them any less
of a strain. Ill health and frequent stays in the hospital,
painful operations and long, lonely post-operative re-
coveries deaden the spirit. Just being instantly cata-
logued as "an old geezer" or "little old lady" by every
younger person you meet is hard on the pride. Even
if people don't literally push you around, they tend
to dismiss you, ignore you, and, worst of all, think
that just because you're old and a little hard of hearing and perhaps a tiny bit forgetful, that you are a
stupid, senile old idiot.

Old age is not without its rewards for many, but for
far more it is a time of accelerating stress. Friends die;
brothers and sisters and relatives die; wives and
husbands, lifetime companions and pillars of support

die. Circumstances conspire and compound your grief. Finances can become crucial; soaring property taxes force you from your home; you have to give up the mobility and independence of driving your own car; your children grow impatient with both your infirmity and your attempts to explain your feelings and concerns; you may have to move into a nursing home which proves to be a season in hell. And, finally, there is death itself, the final, most frightening stress of life, dogging your every waking hour and haunting your dreams.

Seasonal Stress

Such are the changing seasons of stress in contemporary American life. They come with the territory we inhabit in every phase of existence. But there are many special stresses, as well, which we will look at next. One other generic stress needs noting here. It is seasonal in nature and has the virtue of fading away like Halley's Comet, only to return again. Holidays are a prime example—particularly Christmas with its demands that we all somehow find the extra time, money and energy to satisfy expectations great and small. By some great national consensus, the holiday season is the one time in the year when you can't say, "I'll do it next week," or simply, "To hell with it." It requires emotional energy, as well, and for many, long journeys by air, bus, train and car, usually in lousy weather. It's the time when we all "tag up" with the people who are important in our lives.

Like long-planned vacations, another harbinger of

seasonal stress, we pin all our hopes and emotional needs on the holidays and researchers have found that the subsequent stress can produce headaches, stiffness, indigestion and not a little depression. Those who are lonely feel particularly afflicted at this time of year when their condition is seemingly accented and derided by the massive national togetherness spree.

In a story on the subject which appeared in *USA Today*, Steven Helschien of the Helschien Health Center in Columbia, MO, says that "the holiday season is really a high pressure time in most people's lives." Failed expectations, lack of hoped for family harmony and spending beyond limits can make it "a real lonely time psychologically." Add rich foods, late hours and booze and "the holiday season plays havoc on the system," he says.

Marriage and Family Life

Well, it would be nice to have somebody on your side after a long day in the snakepits, right? Marriage and co-habitation have been the traditional results of that basic yearning to incorporate the soothing (stress relieving) elements of companionship, mutual caring, love and sexual satisfaction into our lives.

Few people get married out of a conscious need to relieve stress, of course. Most have far more romantic things in mind. And, in spite of all we've been hearing about the imminent collapse of marriage and family life, the number of marriages and births in this country is on the rise. Marriage and family life still offer tremendous emotional rewards. It is also entered into with unrealistically high hopes on the parts of many—especially young people between 18 and 23, whose marriages collapse at a far higher rate than those who are a bit older.

All married couples experience stress, of course, and each spouse probably has his or her own main culprit. But what are the most frequently cited stresses which people associate with even happy and stable marriages? In her fine book, *Stress and the Healthy Family* (Winston Press, $13.85) columnist and family expert Dolores Curran, who gathered her data from family therapists, counselors and parents, came up with a list of today's ten leading family stresses:

1. Economics/finances/budgeting
2. Children's behavior/discipline/sibling fighting
3. Insufficient couple time
4. Lack of shared repsonsibility in the family
5. Communicating with children
6. Insufficient 'Me' time
7. Guilt for not accomplishing more
8. Spousal relationship (communications, friendship, sex)
9. Insufficient family play time
10. Overscheduled family calendar.

Living Together

The latest figures released by the United States Census Bureau show that the number of unmarried women and men living together has tripled since 1970. Young Americans are postponing marriage for a variety of reasons, including the rising cost of housing, fear of becoming part of the soaring divorce rate, employment problems and the rewards of continuing education on the graduate level. According to the Bureau, there were 523,000 unmarried couples living together in 1970 compared to 1,988,000 such households in March, 1984. There is now even an official acronym for this growing segment of the population: POSSLQ-People of the Opposite Sex Sharing Living Quarters.

Viva la Revolution?

The widely heralded Sexual Revolution has certainly played its part in this dramatic turning away from marriage (though it is actually more of a postponement of marriage and family commitments than an abandonment of them). If nothing else, it has greatly eased the old stigma of scandal about living together out of wedlock. We now read about such couples in the media without raising an eyebrow. And, in some cases, with a touch of envy of the liberated life-style implied by being in a situation which can be terminated instantly and presumably without regret by either party. Also, presumably, the heavy stresses of pregnancy and child-rearing are avoided in such casual arrangements.

However, as many POSSLQs have learned the hard way—particularly women—there are some very real draw-backs to intimacy outside of marriage. Not every

woman has resorted to filing a "Palimony" suit to try
to gain redress from a man who has dumped her ar-
bitrarily for a new and often younger companion, but
there are increasing numbers of them giving voice to
their disenchantment. And these are women who have
enjoyed a relatively long-term relationship, even if it
turned sour and empty for them at the end. They must
always live with the anxiety of possible rejection. Married women have to consider the possibility of divorce,
of course, but they have solid rights under the law,
whereas their unmarried counterparts are far more apt
to be left with nothing to show for "the best years of
their lives" except a battered ego.

Nor has the sexual emancipation of the 60s and 70s
delivered the happiness implicit in its promise of sex
without messy commitment. Its mystique has been
shattered not only by the far messier risks of herpes
and AIDS, but by deep-seated human needs and emotions which, when thwarted, leave both men and
women living in a state of frustration.

In spite of the 1984 Census Bureau figures, there
is growing evidence that the Sexual Revolution may
have peaked and is now subsiding. A *Time* cover story
pronounced that it is, in fact, over, and that in the 80s,
"caution and commitment are the watchwords. From
cities, suburbs and small towns alike, there is growing evidence that the national obsession with sex is
subsiding." The article quotes a New York City writer
who slept with about two dozen women in the months
following his divorce: "It's terrible to wake up and
wonder why this person's head is on the other pillow.
It was painful for them and for me, too." And a

Chicago bar owner reports: "All the happy-go-lucky singles in my place tell me they do not want a relationship. Then six months later they are engaged."

Nationally syndicated columnist Ann Landers, whose voluminous incoming mail amounts to an ongoing social survey of the manners and mores of the nation, says that she is hearing more and more about the disappointments and stresses of liberated women who have opted for a life of casual sex rather than the "exploitation" of marriage, childbearing and housework. They write that they end up feeling just as "used" even if they don't risk pregnancy. They risk so many other things and receive so little emotional satisfaction that their lives are not only filled with anxiety but their sense of well boing and self esteem plunges to zero. And, after an initial burst of cooperation in sharing domestic chores on the part of their male companions, many find themselves doing as much housework as married women.

According to *Newsweek*, a growing number of unmarried couples are turning to professional counseling to iron out conflicts and clarify relationships which grow out of living together for extended periods in the absence of a formal commitment. Often, one party is consciously or unconsciously seeking to formalize their union through marriage, while the other is just as reluctant to do so as he or she was when the couple first became lovers.

Reports Newsweek: "Psychologist Robert Resnick of Santa Monica, California, estimates that up to seventy percent of his unmarried clients, with particular stresses and strains of their own, are already living together. For one thing, notes Jay Haley, director of Washington's Family Therapy Institute, 'they can't rely on the traditional script' for solving their problems. Even though the practice is now widely accepted, living together may still be taboo in the eyes of their parents. 'There's not even a language for it,' says Haley. 'Are you a lover? Are you a roommate? It can get pretty confusing.' "

Divorce

Divorce is among the oldest solutions to the stress of a marriage gone sour. What is new is that so many people are invoking it these days. In the early 1950s, about 350,000 people were separated legally by the divorce courts of the United States. In 1982, some 1.2 million Americans divorced each other. That staggering figure actually reflected a slight drop from the previous year's total—the first decline in 20 years. In the same year, according to the National Center for Health's statistics, a record 2.5 million couples married. If the figures balance out it means that unless the decline in divorce accelerates radically, almost half of those who married in 1982 will eventually get divorced.

Meant to ease pain and stress, divorce, as all too many have discovered, can open up a whole new dimension of stress and emotional anguish. These could be and have been the subject of many a book-length study. I won't rehash them here except to note that there are millions among us who carry those extra and often searing stresses around with them every day of their lives in addition to whatever other stresses they must deal with. Many will re-marry and a goodly percentage will get divorced again, adding to the already constant simmer of stress. Serial marriages, tiers of children born of these several unions, complex economic support arrangements, all are increasingly common on the American scene and all pose new stress variations that are not susceptible to quick or easy relief.

Single Parents

Being a single parent is often an additional stress, a "fringe benefit," of divorce. The majority of single parents are women, many of whom also have full time jobs. But a surprising number of single dads are now taking on the parental role, as well. In 1983 there were some 600,000 divorced and separated men raising children under 18—an increase over 1970 figures of 180 percent.

In addition to assuming the total burden of child care, providing meals, health care, clothing and handling all household chores on a solo basis, single parents who must be both mother and father carry a burden of concern about their children's whereabouts and safety during the hours that they are not in day care centers or at school. They also face additional stress on the job, since it is sometimes necessary to be late for work, to have to leave early and sometimes miss a day or more altogether. And, of course, their social lives have to be elaborately structured and scheduled if they are ever to get out of the pressure cooker at all.

HOW I RELAX

Alas, there is no one formula for dealing with stress —at least none that I have discovered. Perhaps this is because my anxieties run the range from mere dislike of a task to deep and terrifying entrapment in situations that seem to have no solution. The prospect of an unpleasant day offers one kind of stress. The critical illness of a little child is an entirely different matter. Surely the quality of the emotion in each instance is different.

I can generally handle minor anxieties by thinking of of something pleasant that I can do at the end of the day—reading a good book or dinner with family or friends. The pleasant thought seems to be enough to get me moving. As for "catastrophic concerns," I have learned to pose a challenge. I simply ask myself: Are you a coward? To date I have been able to come up with the appropriate answer.

Rabbi Robert J. Marx
Hakafa Congregation, Glencoe, IL
Founder of the Jewish Council
on Urban Affairs

The Delayed Stress Syndrome

Researchers are currently exploring yet another sort of stress which has been around for a long time but which has only recently been singled out and identified. The delayed stress syndrome manifests itself in people who have undergone relatively long periods of intense anxiety and fear. They somehow had to continue to function under terrible conditions and the experience replays later, sometimes over and over, in terms of stressful feelings which can range from anxiety attacks to acute depression. Combat veterans who used to be called victims of "shell shock" are actually suffering from the delayed stress syndrome. Thousands who fought in Viotnam for prolonged periods are still victims, as are a mounting number of surviving hostages and others who have lived through traumatic instances of international terrorism.

Uli Derikson, the heroic stewardess who underwent the tension-wracked two-day ordeal of the June, 1985, Middle East hijacking of TWA's flight 847, told *People* magazine that while she required little in the way of psychological support in the weeks immediately following her release, she has had a dream in which she saw the hijackers on her porch and is having difficulty overcoming the anxiety that is triggered whenever she encounters a bearded, dark Middle Eastern-looking man. "When I see somebody in the airport who has that profile, I am very uneasy." She is determined to put the whole experience out of her mind: "Life goes on and I'm trying to put 847 on the back burner. This is the year it happened and this will be the year we finish with it."

Let's hope so for her sake, but many victims of delayed stress are finding it more tenaciously long-lasting than a few months or even years.

Technostress

Finally, there is a totally new form of stress which is making its presence felt in homes and offices around the country. In his book, *Technostress: The Human Cost of the Computer Revolution* (Addision-Wesley, $16.30) psychologist Craig Brod defines technostress as a "modern disease of adaption caused by an inability to cope with the new technologies in a healthy manner."

In one form it afflicts those who have an innate fear of computers and other electronic marvels which have already, or threaten to disrupt the work patterns of a lifetime, and may appear job-threatening. It is this sort of "technoanxiety" which overtakes not just clerical workers and managers who find themselves suddenly surrounded by mysterious machines, but by a new breed of co-workers who appear totally at ease and expert with them. The threatened individual perceives himself or herself (with some accuracy) as being pushed further and further to the perimeter of the work scene. And it is not stretching things too much to note that, just as insurance salesmen have always used the thinly veiled threat of what will happen when the bread-winner of a family dies as the ultimate reason for paying out large policy premiums, the purveyors of home computers imply that if you don't get one of their machines in your house that your children will grow up to be techno-illiterates.

In a feature story on technostress, Ellen Jaffe McClain of News America Syndicate says that, in his book, Brod is primarily concerned with the "techno-centered individual," the person who has mastered the new technology but who then begins to identify with the computer itself, right up to the point that she or he becomes machinelike in behavior and appears cut off from human interaction and emotion. "Signs of the technocentered state include a high degree of factual thinking, poor access to feelings, an insistence on efficiency and speed, a lack of empathy for others and a low tolerance for the ambiguities of human behavior and communication," says Brod.

Eventually, writes McClain, "the technocentered worker becomes just as tired, physically and mentally, as someone struggling to master the new machine. He or she begins to have difficulty calculating, planning, making decisions and keeping track of time. Once home, the technocentered person makes a lousy parent, spouse or lover, impatient with questions that require more than yes and no answers, and wanting only to be left alone."

Other researchers are concerned with the physical stressors of the new generation of computerized offices. The increased productivity made possible by computers, laser printers, modems, copiers and the like, often make it possible to reduce an office staff so that an increased work load is actually being handled by fewer people. Long hours in front of Video Display Terminals brings on eye-strain, sore backs, fatigue and illness. Eventually, the toll mounts and productivity drops off sharply. Some states are already considering laws which would set limits on consecutive VDT hours and mandate rest breaks and time for some interaction with fellow workers. Studies have confirmed that productivity increases once again and absenteeism declines when such human factors are introduced.

HOW I RELAX

For odd moment, break-in-the-day relaxing, I always have a book in my handbag. If I have to wait at someone's desk; if I go to the washroom; when I have a skim-milk lunch at my desk—I find that even five minutes reading in my chosen book is noticeably relaxing.

I usually have trouble getting to sleep. There is, however, a routine (I suppose a form of self-hypnosis) that always seems to work. It is not something I originated; I read about it years ago. One imagine's, in the mind's eye, an individual writing on a blackboard. One has to concentrate until one sees the hand holding the chalk actually writing, not a "picture" of the writing, but the visualization of fingers holding the chalk and the chalk moving over the board developing the writing. One usually does not stay awake long enough to actually see what is being written.

At various times in the past four years or so, when I have been under severe strain of nervous tension, I have experienced brief symptoms that automatically make me think "heart attack." I have just as automatically started deep breathing and sort of "talking" to my heart. In some doubtlessly irrational way I have this gut feeling that the heart will respond if I maintain a forceful rhythm of breathing. Irrational or not, this technique does seem to alleviate or at least control the extreme stress symptoms.

Anne Coyne
Teacher
Washburne Trade School
Chicago Board of Education

CHAPTER FOUR
Stress and Consequences

IN the introduction, stress was defined in a general way as any disturbance, strain, stimulus or interference that upsets the functioning of mind or body. That it certainly is, but if we are to truly understand the way stress works its pervasive way with us—and we must have at least a glimmer of knowledge if we are to successfully deal with it—we need to look at it more closely.

What Is Stress?

Hans Selye, the famed Viennese-born doctor who first formulated the revolutionary concept of the stress syndrome, defines stress as *"the nonspecific response of the body to any demand, whether it is caused by, or results in, pleasant or unpleasant conditions."* In this admittedly technical definition, stress, as such, is all-inclusive, both positive and negative. Good things, exciting things, pleasant things, which he calls *eustress* cause the body to undergo the same sort of nonspecific responses as do the bad or negative things, which he calls *distress*.

Both *eustress* (from the Greek "eu," or good) and *distress* (from the Latin, "dis," or bad) he calls *stressors*. The important thing to understand, however difficult this is to do when in the grips of stress, is that of themselves these *stressors* are, by and large, "neutral." It is how we "take," or interpret them, that sets off the stress syndrome.

Seyle, who conducted elaborate experiments with animals as well as years of other research, reached this conclusion by observing that while both negative and positive *stressors* triggered definite (though varying) physical reactions, those resulting from *eustress* caused much less long-term damage to the organism than those resulting from *distress*. Furthermore, since stress is a syndrome, it results in a group of changes, not just a single reaction. This is what he means by nonspecific. If you burn your hand bad things happen to its skin and nerves and you experience pain, but this is not stress in our meaning. If you get tripped up in a soccer game, bruise your knee, and jump up determined not only to get even but to run rings around the opponents, scoring goal after goal while the crowd cheers you wildly, this is stimulation, not stress.

To sum up by way of oversimplified example, it is not the fact that your car overheats and stalls leaving you stranded and helpless in the middle of the expressway that is stress. A dead motor is simply a dead motor. What causes stress reactions to be triggered is your perception that: you have been left in a very dangerous situation; you have already been late to your new job once already this week and the boss doesn't seem to like you and is looking for an excuse to get rid of you; you just spent $135 on a tune-up last week and were obviously ripped off; you really need a new car even though your credit is extended to its limit and you are paying exorbitant interest rates to nurse it along; you're now going to have to pay an outrageous sum to an emergency tow truck, if and when one finds you; and if and when you do finally get to work, you're going to be so shook up that you will make a thorough mess of the report which you have to have in by lunch.

This is part of what Seyle calls the "stress of living," and it is not of itself physical. It is in the mind of the individual who perceives it as it affects him or her. Obviously it is being taken very distressfully by the person in our example. In his mind it touches many things that are threatening and negative. But, while nobody gets a kick out of stalling out in a traffic jam, it's not difficult to place another individual in the same scenario who will perceive it merely as an inconvenience—a well-to-do retired tourist, perhaps, with nothing but time on his hands and no job or financial pressures. To him it's an inconvenience, to be sure, but one that will soon be resolved without further stressful consequences.

So we have the same event perceived by two different minds. If you will accept a non-scientific distinction here between "mind" and "brain," it may help to gain an insight into the nature of stress which will be useful: a mind belongs to an individual and is the sum of his or her knowledge and experience— no two are alike; the brain is an essential component of the mind but it is (with certain differences in capacity, etc.) generic to all human beings. Provided with similar stimuli, human brains will more or less react in the same fashion. This is tricky because in one sense, the mind seems to reside in one part of the brain —the cortex—but the cortex never has the last say, or ultimate control, since it cannot exist apart from the rest of the brain. The point here is simply that two minds perceive and interpret the same negative stressor in very different ways and send off different sets of stimuli to their respective brains.

With this distinction, however crudely stated, in mind, we can gain further insights into the true nature of stress from some more recent and down-to-earth definitions of it. Dr. Barbara B. Brown, pioneer in the field of biofeedback (and the person who named this technique for coping with stress) defines it in her highly regarded book *Between Health & Illness: New Notions on Stress and the Nature of Well Being:* "The 'stress of life' is *not* physical stress. Stress as we talk about it today, is the special pressure people feel as they face difficulties in life and as they interact with the inventions of people, such as business, politics, sports or love. Stress grows from social situations and the psychological reactions they create. It is psychic trauma, never physical trauma." Dr. Floyd E. Bloom of Scripps Clinic and Research, La Jolla, Ca., puts it even more simply: "Anxiety and stress are the buffer between an event in the world which I must interpret and the way I'm going to interpret it."

How Stress Affects Us

In spite of enormous scientific strides, the human brain may still be accurately described as one of nature's last frontiers. We know that all human behavior is controlled by the brain and that it operates not randomly but by intricate chemical and electrical processes, a very few of which researchers have charted.

HOW I RELAX

First of all, I say my prayers daily—Mass, Breviary and others—so at least I get through the day knowing that I am depending on God and not upon myself. I realize that something is required of me, but that is easier if I can assume God's help through prayer.

Secondly, I never carry one form of problem into another that follows. In other words, I do what I have to when I am doing it and I don't worry about what I have just done or what I have ahead of me. In this way, I can give full attention to each problem as it occurs. I also don't take problems to bed with me at night and, over the past thirty years, full of multitudinous problems each day, I have rarely had difficulty getting to sleep quickly. Part of that might also be due to the fact that I pray the Rosary in bed, and that has the same effect spiritually that reciting a mantra might have in another context.

Lastly, I refuse to worry. I don't think any problem is solved more easily if one worries about it. In fact, I think worry is a useless form of human activity, always harmful rather than helpful. I do all that I can and let the Lord help me with the rest. Worrying would only complicate the situation. One's peace of mind is terribly important, especially if one is facing endless days of crisis, problems and highly charged activity, such as decision-making, constant speeches and a variety of interpersonal relationships.

Rev. Theodore M. Hesburgh
President
University of Notre Dame

But, since there are some fifty billion brain cells and each of them is interacting or being acted upon by thousands of others—even when we sleep—our deepest feelings, things like love and hate, our sense of identity, and much more, may always remain a mystery.

But, thanks to the work of Seyle and others, we do know something about the emotion of anxiety which is caused by perceived stress, and what the brain experiencing it does to the body.

One way to approach it is to go back in time—to a time when earliest humans, *homo sapiens*, struggled for survival in a far less complex world than ours. We could perhaps make the same case with an animal today, but it is thinking man, not an imperiled bullfrog who is our ancestor. So, while the description of what happens when any animal is suddenly threatened with termination is just as apt for imperiled humans, there were, from the beginning, some important differences.

We are talking about the most basic of reactions —fight or flight. Immediate physical threat always provokes this response in an animal or in a human. A chipmunk, though instinctively wary, doesn't sit around in its hole worrying about owls or cats or snakes it may encounter the next day. A caveman who had seen the tracks of a saber-toothed tiger in his vicinity during the morning and who heard it roaring in the distance at night, grew anxious—with good reason. He interpreted these signals, these *stressors*, as potentially life-threatening. Though not under immediate threat, his thinking mind, the part of him that had seen and recorded all the woeful varieties of damage that a saber-toothed tiger can inflict, sent out the same signals, only slightly less imperative than if the tiger was about to spring at him, to prepare to fight for his life or run like hell.

His brain, already marvelous in its mysterious complexity, formulated and transmitted the necessary electrical and chemical signals for meeting such a challenge. The central nervous system is put into high gear; blood pressure and heart rate increase in anticipation of exertion; a neuro-transmitter is released by the hypothalamus, which in turn causes the pituitary gland, the adrenal gland and the locus coeruleus to release the necessary chemicals to put his body at the highest level of readiness. Coagulants are released into the bloodstream in anticipation of bleeding from wounds, while the blood itself retreats from more vulnerable extremities such as hands and feet to the relative safety of internal organs. Maximum sharpness and field of vision are called for, so the pupils of the eyes dilate. In fact, all the senses get sharper; extraneous thoughts are dangerous distractions, so the pattern of the brain's waves change. There's even more, but you get the picture.

Fortunately for the caveman, there were only so many saber-toothed tigers in the world, and he soon discovered that he was wilier than all of them put together. But the fact remains that lots of very complex things happened to his body when under the fight or flight stress they triggered in him. Obviously, one can't remain at that peak of utter physical and psychological readiness for prolonged periods. Presently, when no tiger actually showed up, his body retreated from this stage of what Seyle calls "the alarm reaction" to a "resistance stage." In this state he was still alert, still revved up chemically, but other concerns return to mind, things like getting some food, making a fire, getting on with essentials intrude. But the stress alert is still on, still lurking just beneath the surface of consciousness. Finally, unless the caveman succeeds in relaxing and forgetting all about the tiger, he may succumb to the "exhaustion stage," in which he runs the risk of becoming ill.

Seyle structured all these aspects of stress into something he calls the "General Adaption Syndrome" (GAS). It is his conviction that we cope with stress by using up "adaptive" or coping energy. Nor does he forget that much of life's stress is not only unavoidable but necessary. It's what keeps us moving, meets deadlines, spurs us to achievement, provides us with the highs which are the spice of life, keeps us out of ruts—in short, makes us human instead of animals or vegetables (turnips experience no stress whatsoever).

But either way, in *eustress* or *distress* we are constantly using up adaptive energy in our struggle to cope with stress and its effect on our bodies. Seyle credits us all with an hereditary fund of "deep adaptive energy," a reserve which varies and however well-funded, is capable of depletion; "superficial adaptive energy" is what we draw on from day-to-day. It can be replenished, but if it isn't, it will eventually bite into and exhaust the hereditary store and leave us bankrupt and vulnerable to the long-range ravages of stress related woes.

Brilliant as his insights and finds are, Dr. Seyle would probably admit that things may not be quite so cut and dried as that. Even with what we know, we are still only on the threshold of understanding why stress affects us as it does and, more importantly, why living the full life, living up to full potential in the fast track, is itself dangerous to living. Many who have continued Dr. Seyle's work feel that our ability to cope with stress has evolved along with the rest of our physical and psychological refinements. Humankind remains the most adapatable of creatures (though not necessarily the longest-lasting) by virtue of our brains. A caveman set down in the middle of one of today's cities would probably "stress out" in a matter of hours. Still, given the incredible acceleration of change and the geometrical expansion of stressors thrust upon us in the past fifty years alone, it's virtually a certainty that our innate ability to cope with stress is lagging dangerously far behind what it needs to be.

As stress researcher Dr. Jay Weiss of New York's Rockefeller University sums it up: "Life was probably no picnic for the caveman, but my guess is that he didn't produce at the rate we produce in Western industrialized culture from nine to five P.M. My guess is that he slept a fair percentage of that time and he sure didn't worry about it in the evening when he went home to watch TV. So my conjecture would be that our major problem is that we drive ourselves too hard."

The Bottom Line

We laypeople, victims of stress though we may be, don't really have to throw ourselves onto the cutting

HOW I RELAX

Sometimes I just take a deep breath and give myself 30 seconds of perspective. I'm likely to tell myself such things as, "In the overall scheme of things..." or, "Someday this will be funny..." or, "Don't let the bastards get you down." If it's more than a momentary annoyance, I may take a few more minutes and concentrate on tension in my body. Sometimes I visualize muscles, veins, etc., and watch them relax, concentrate on feeling them relax. If I'm in an excessively long or boring meeting, I go on fantasy trips.

The point is that I have kept my blood pressure low and my sometimes cheery disposition by trying to keep a little distance from many of the day-to-day hassles. My friends would probably tell you that I don't do a very good job of it. I seem always to be outraged about some injustice or stomping and screaming passionately about one cause or another. But, believe me, I practice a lot of self control and "relaxation" stuff. Lord knows what I'd be like if I didn't.

As for more serious stuff like spending an evening resting or going to sleep, I watch "MASH" and "Barney Miller" reruns, lie in hot tubs, exercise moderately (walk, bicycle) and sometimes, if sleep is a problem, do a thing that a shrink friend taught me: get comfortable, relax the body one section at a time, then take a mental walk through a beautiful garden with wonderful smells, sights, sounds, tastes, feelings. When you take the same walk repeatedly it seems to get more familiar, pleasant and gratifying.

The imaging is especially helpful when I'm dieting. I'm one of those people who has lost 200 pounds in the last ten years—the same 20 pounds every year. It helps me practice self-control when I get a mental picture of what I'll look like if I hang in. But the technique helps with stress management, too. In times of stress, I think about a period when I was happy, high, competent, full-functioning—try to see what I looked like—and the positive feelings seep through to the present.

Frances Morris
Columnist, Television Personality
Assistant Clincial Professor of Psychiatry
and Behavioral Science, University of Oklahoma

edge of the continuing scientific research and debate
about the precise way stress affects the brain and how
the brain affects our bodies. It is hard not to agree with
Dr. Barbara Brown's conclusion that modern humans
don't react to the psychological and emotional stressors that are our main bugbears in the same way that
the caveman responded to the tiger at his door. When
the letter informing us that the IRS is holding a little
audit party in our honor we don't drop into a protec-
tive crouch, break out in a cold sweat and dilate our
pupils, even though we might like to.

Dr. Brown feels that our brains have come a long
way in learning to adapt to and cope with all sorts
of non-physical (social) hazards by employing our
thought processes to deal with them successfully.
And, when you think about it, all of us negotiate a
mine-field of such obstacles and emotional hazards
each day. We don't just pull up short and wring our
hands about every big and little set-back. We have
long since developed mental strategies and alternatives which, either from experience or from the wisdom and experience of others, enable us to deal with
or avoid stressors which would have sent our caveman
up the wall.

But it's nonetheless true that, as Dr. Weiss says, "we
drive ourselves too hard"—ours (and society's) expectations as we perceive them are overwhelming; the
acceleration of change, of lifestyles, of opportunities,
of potential conflicts and frustrations still far outstrip
our mind's ability to cope with them. When these
stressors, whether perceived and interpreted as excit-
ingly good or bad are accepted into our consciousness

(and there's really no way we can keep them out) an imbalance between the thinking part of the brain and the emotional part results. And when that happens all sorts of physical and chemical changes in the body result. These changes, however varied and however relatively severe, place a strain on our nervous system, our cardiovascular system, and on various organs, including the heart. This is not sickness, this is stress. And stress, as we shall see, can be a stimulant, a mild irritant, and all too often, a killer.

Public Enemy Number One: Stress

As noted earlier, worrying is modern America's most popular indoor sport. In particular, worrying about health, fitness and disease. As this is being written AIDS is very much on the national mind. Cancer and heart disease are only temporarily overshadowed. There is new hope for a preventative measure that will wipe out the common cold. Before AIDS, polio was the great mystery menace—children were kept apart; swimming pools were closed. Flu in all its varieties causes periodic panics which are fueled by the terrible carnage of the 1918 epidemic which killed hundreds of thousands around the world. Tuberculosis, with good reason, was for centuries the most dreaded and mysterious of afflictions. Smallpox, cholera, malaria, bubonic and other virulent plagues took fearsome tolls.

Some brilliant medical breakthroughs have disposed of most these killers. Improved knowledge about bacteria, viruses and the widespread implementation of public sanitation standards based upon this knowledge have rendered most of these menaces far less widespread and lethal, at least in the industrialized world. But as they have receded they have gradually made room for light to reveal an almost invisible (because so well camoflaged) killer that is more deadly than many of the others combined ever were. It is a malady which is transmitted by no germs or viruses, against which there are no vaccines, which afflicts virtually everyone at some time in their life, and many for most of their lives, which is so sneaky and varied in its manifestations that it is seldom detected before it has caused severe damage, and which can kill in a dazzling variety of ways.

Stress is the affliction of the twentieth century. Experts agree that on the conservative end of the scale stress is the principal or chief contributing cause of 70 percent of all illnesses today—some say 90 percent. The fact that stress itself is not a disease, but rather a *dis-ease* that causes disease, is more than a semantic distinction—it's what makes stress so sneaky and so very pervasive.

On the less malignant side of the scale, stress triggers or worsens such problems as chronic exhaustion and anxiety. It keeps thousands of us in that state where we aren't exactly sick but in which we never, or all too seldom, wake up feeling "on top of the world." Headaches which seem utterly unrelated to colds or eye-strain or backed up sinuses have stress written all over them, not EXCEDRIN. Stress can affect our ability to think clearly and to remember accurately; it keeps us awake at night and, having absolutely no sense of decency, it can interfere with our sex lives by killing off libido and even causing impotency.

Stress can make us eat and drink too much—which in turn causes more physical stress on our bodies; it is stress that keeps too many of us poking cigarettes, pipes and chewing tobacco in our mouths. Even without the unhealthful consequences of these destructive coping devices which we employ in an effort to squirm from beneath relentless pressure of stress, its constant flow of chemical signals from our chronically over-excited brains can release adrenalin, cholesterol and all sorts of other inappropriate but potent juices, including bile, which bring on high blood pressure, jangling nerves, ulcers, burning eyes, and generally keep us at such a boil that we actually age faster.

Psychologically, stress can make us edgy, hostile, anti-social (even criminal), depressed and even suicidal.

Finally, there's convincing evidence that prolonged stress, by compounding all of the above, leads to angina, heart failure, and yes, even to cancer, because it ultimately affects the body's immune protection system adversely.

Measuring Stress

How much stress is too much? Is there any way to measure something so intangible? Veteran stress researchers Thomas H. Holmes and Richard Rahe of the University of Washington School of Medicine developed a method of measuring the stresses caused by life changes—good and bad—in a controlled group of naval personnel. Men who scored high on their scale experienced nearly 90 percent more illnesses than those on the low end of it. Though it should be regarded as a relative guide, you may wish to see how your life in the past year adds up.

SOCIAL READJUSTMENT RATING SCALE

Circle each "life event" that has occurred within the past year. If a particular item has been repeated, you may count it more than once.

Life Event	Mean Value
1. Death of spouse	100
2. Divorce	73
3. Marital separation from mate	65
4. Detention in jail or other institution	63
5. Death of a close family member	63
6. Major personal injury or illness	53
7. Marriage	50
8. Being fired at work	47
9. Marital reconciliation with mate	45
10. Retirement from work	45
11. Major change in the health or behavior of a family member	44
12. Pregnancy	40

13. Sexual difficulties   39

14. Gaining a new family member (e.g.,   39
    through birth, adoption, oldster
    moving in, etc.)

15. Major business readjustment (e.g.,   39
    merger, reorganization, bankruptcy,
    etc.)

16. Major change in financial state (e.g.,   38
    a lot worse off or a lot better off
    than usual)

17. Death of a close friend   37

18. Changing to a different line of work   36

19. Major change in the number of argu-   35
    ments with spouse (e.g., either a lot
    more or a lot less than usual regard-
    ing childrearing, personal habits,
    etc.)

20. Taking on a mortgage greater than   31
    $10,000 (e.g., purchasing home,
    business, etc.)

21. Foreclosure on a mortgage or loan   30

22. Major change in responsibilities at   29
    work (e.g., promotion, demotion,
    lateral transfer)

23. Son or daughter leaving home (e.g.,   29
    marriage, attending college, etc.)

24. In-law troubles 29

25. Outstanding personal achievement 28

26. Spouse beginning or ceasing work outside the home 26

27. Beginning or ceasing formal schooling 26

28. Major change in living conditions (e.g., building a new home, remodeling, deterioration of home or neighborhood) 25

29. Revision of personal habits (e.g., dress, manner associations, etc.) 24

30. Troubles with the boss 23

31. Major change in working hours or conditions 20

32. Change in residence 20

33. Changing to a new school 20

34. Major change in usual type and/or amount of recreation 19

35. Major change in church activities (e.g., a lot more or a lot less than usual) 19

36. Major change in social activities   18
    (e.g., clubs, dancing, movies, visit-
    ing, etc.)

37. Taking on a mortgage or a loan less   17
    than $10,000 (e.g., purchasing a car,
    TV, freezer, etc.)

38. Major change in sleeping habits   16
    (e.g., a lot more or a lot less sleep,
    or change in part of day when
    asleep)

39. Major change in number of family   15
    get-togethers (e.g., a lot more or a
    lot less than usual)

40. Major change in eating habits (e.g.,   15
    a lot more or a lot less food intake,
    or very different meal hours or sur-
    roundings)

41. Vacation   13

42. Christmas   12

43. Minor violations of the law (e.g.,   11
    traffic tickets, jaywalking, disturbing
    the peace, etc.)

Total life change unit values: _____

Interpreting your score:

150-199 = You have a mild chance of incurring some kind of health change (surgery, illness, accident, psychiatric disorder) in the next year.

200-299 = You are a moderate risk.

Over 300 = You are very likely to suffer a major physical or emotional illness.

* * *

How Stress Gets Away with Murder

If these statistics, and these only partially chronicled destructive disturbances, can all be laid on stress's doorstep, why isn't medical science doing more about it? Millions are being spent on cancer and cardiac research, not to mention specific cures for dozens of other diseases which afflict a relative few compared to the millions caught up in the progressive grip of stress-related afflictions.

The answer is that medical science is indeed paying more attention to stress and to stress regulation and alleviation. The whole health care establishment is beginning to take stress and the harmful coping habits and life-styles it engenders very much into consideration. The problem is extremely complex, however. First of all, there's no way anyone can mount a successful campaign to immunize humankind against "the stress of life." If it manifests itself in widespread destructive behaviors which foster disease in many varieties, it's quite possible to treat the diseases but not the cause. What is possible, and what is slowly being accomplished, is to make people more aware of the fact that they need not compound their stress by harmful coping behaviors and that it is possible to regulate and even minimize the effects of stress.

Until now, medicine could only intervene after stress had festered long enough to cause recognizable symptoms and damage. And there can never be a "cure" for stress because it has no physical cause. So, short of putting the majority of the adult population of the country on powerful tranquilizers, medical science can only do so much. And much of that "so much" will take the form of education, in sharing the findings of its researchers in ways which laypeople can understand and act upon.

We will look at the ways in which you can do just that in the next chapter. It is true that you cannot avoid the "stress of living," but it does not have to destroy you.

HOW I RELAX

Everyone's biological clock is, they say, as personal as fingerprints or voiceprints. To describe how to minimize stress, then, might be to give answers to unasked questions, or prescriptions where there is no disease. Yet one hears enough about the need to compensate for too-short nights of sleep, and to idle the mental motor, to encourage me to pass on word about how I do it.

Evidently, I am considered an expert on the subject. When "the fifteen minutes of celebrity," which Andy Warhol predicts for all of us, came to me in the form of a write-up in *People* magazine, the main picture was a full page spread of me—napping. Characteristically.

If you're interested, here's how one person does it, and teaches others, sometimes with success, to do this mental motor idling. Personal adaptions may be necessary.

1. Never nap more than fifteen minutes. You fall into a deep sleep and wake up dopey. The point is merely to drop off.

2. While in training, take the phone off the hook— this is vital, since the possibility of its ringing can keep you awake—and put a record on the player. Serene classical music, not Hayden's "Surprise Symphony," or crashing cymbals. It should be loud enough to drown out distracting noises. After a while you won't need music. You can drop off in Grand

Central Station—but not in the beginning stages.

3. Find a good floor, or a couch. Use a book or a coat for a pillow. Flop down.

4. Clear your mind. If you are a Christian—I suppose I could find theological approaches for others, too, such as Buddhists, but they're supposed to be better at this in the first place than others—you may have to do some Christian exercises. It's my theory that what keeps us awake and stressful is guilt about yesterday and worry about tomorrow. Turn the guilt over to God. God accepts the unacceptable. You are unacceptable. God is gracious. Dietrich Bonhoeffer worried about cheap grace. Maybe this is cheap grace. Worry about handling that when you are not trying to nap.

Oh, yes, worry: mention of it is to turn to tomorrow. In this case, remember the Sermon on the Mount and the Lord's Prayer. You are commanded not to worry. Be obedient. Allow yourself to worry after you wake up, if you like to worry. Do without it right now. You are told to pray for daily bread, not tomorrow's. Forget about tomorrow. That's hard to do, since pre-nap time is often given over to setting agendas, planning, being anxious, and when it is thus given over, pre-nap time means non-nap time.

This may sound a bit flip, but I mean it, and it's vital. However you do it, you've now taken care of God by letting God take care of you. You're ready to let technique take over.

5. Here's my technique. I have the unsubstantiable but effective theory that the logic of guilt/worry;

yesterday/tomorrow; regret/plan is all hooked into linear, rational thinking. And that connects, metaphorically and maybe in mental practice, with gravity. So start thinking a-gravitational thoughts. Work hard at not letting anything be anchored, or sized right. Let anything come into mind. The keyhole. Let it become as big as Eliot's "vast, vacant interstellar spaces." Then turn it into a pink cobweb and let it spin. Maybe invent a mantra or short phrase on the spot, and use it for silent incantation. Oh, that cobweb-keyhole is going? Then take a letter of the alphabet, turn it into something fluid, and green, and cosmic, or minuscule; let it wave in the breeze. And it can become something else. Sooner or later a rational, logical, chronological thought will interrupt and you'll get mad. You've lost all your ground. Start over. It's not hard. The second time it will work.

You may have to practice for days, but odds are that it will eventually pay off. If not, you may well have invented your own technique in the meantime.

6. Be sure to have a timer, your watch, or some person's alert system, to awaken you in fifteen minutes—or, in the beginning, trust the sound of the end of the phonograph record to awaken you. You might get up thinking you probably did not drop off today. You probably did, and will feel refreshed. The moment of waking is very cruel, just as it was this morning. You will have an ontological shock. But you get that if you don't nap, or if you nap too long, also. You'll get over it. You'll be refreshed for hours to come. (I try to do this dropping off about twice a day,

for boosts). You can cut an hour or so off your night's sleep, or have more energy to put to work. You can effect more mischief. Or you can induce more boredom by telling everyone what your technique for napping is.

Who knows, I may have done you a service by going on this long when I was asked for a couple of paragraphs. I may have bored you to tears—or to slumber.

Martin E. Marty
Fairfax M. Cone Distinguished Service
Professor of the History of Modern Christianity
The University of Chicago
National Book Award-winning Author

CHAPTER FIVE
Managing Stress

THERE are three basic approaches to coping with the destructive power of prolonged stress:

1. Completely eliminate the stressor;
2. Resist and minimize the stressor;
3. Accept the fact that some stress is inescapable but can be managed and relieved.

In practice, any successful attempt to manage stress will employ all three options.

Eliminating Unnecessary Stress

Remember that while stressors can be physical things such as noise, heat and overcrowding, as well as encounters with people, places and events, the stress syndrome itself (tenseness, pounding heart, headaches, stomachaches, insomnia, nervous irritability, etc.) is triggered by our own mental perception of how these stressors, or combinations thereof, are going to upset our lives, our plans, our hopes, our expectations, our self-image, our happiness and our well-being. Stress is brought on because we don't know how to "fight" these distressing perceptions and we most often cannot "run away" from them (quit the job, hide from creditors, leave school, abandon the handicapped child, or any of the other myriad stressors that we have seen rising out of virtually every stage of life and lifestyle in modern society).

Stress arises and keeps bubbling as long as we see ourselves in a painful or disruptively unsettling situation from which we can hope for no escape. We simply don't know how to cope.

If we did, we would take action to solve the problem. The same brain that is running our stress cooker is also frantically seeking the solution—the information, the knowledge—which will eliminate the stress. More times than most of us give it credit for, it actually does come up with an answer. The sub-conscious mind has been given a bad reputation by many psychiatrists as a breeder of all sorts of complexes, sinister sexual repressions and compensations. Nobody knows for sure how it works, but work it does—relentlessly. And, however it works, it is capable of sorting through all the information available to it not only quickly, but much like a computer, in that it is not distracted by all the sensual bombardment which rains down on the conscious part of our brains.

Most people have had the experience of finally succeeding in consigning a conscious worry or problem to their subconscious mind by saying, "I'll just have to sleep on this one," (or as Scarlet O'Hara kept telling herself in the novel *Gone With the Wind*, "I won't think about that today, I'll think about that tomorrow"), only to wake up the next morning with a solution which pops back into the conscious mind with a triumphant thud.

Still, even the unconscious brain needs knowledge to cope with stress. When it comes, say in the form of a telegram to a distraught parent, with the information that a son in the army long classified as "missing in action" has been located and is alive, the stress syndrome shuts down instantly. The sense of relief is almost dizzying and can, in fact, be just that, as muscles relax, blood pressure drops, veins open, pupils contract.

Or, if a person who perceives himself as being victimized by long-term debt—who has conjured up an image of himself as a hopeless loser in a vicious financial circle from which he can see no escape—suddenly learns of a scheme whereby he can not only consolidate his debts, but actually begin to reduce them, he will (wisely or not) experience this same sort of relief.

In such cases stress has been eliminated because the stressor has been removed, or because an answer, a way to cope has suddenly appeared. Easy, you say, but no such magic wand exists in the case of my stress.

You may be right, but some stressors you are living with as fixtures in your life can be eliminated by a close and honest examination of your priorities and habits (Does your bathroom floor really have to be washed every Saturday morning? Does it bother you all that much that your wife forgets to deduct the checks she writes?) You may also find a substantial number of petty, but nonetheless irritating stressors that have moved into your life years ago and now, in truth, bother you more by past association and habitual annoyance than they do in fact. (The neighbor's dog used to bark and use your patio for its daily duty; it drove you wild; but two years ago the neighbors put up a fence; the dog is older and no longer barks; but it still gives you a spasm every time you see the dog, or even think about it.)

Another tactic, one which most people are reluctant to entertain because it means making changes, is to recognize that a particular stressor can't be removed from your life as it is presently set up, but it doesn't follow that you can't remove yourself from its presence. If your job, your boss, your co-workers are driving you up the wall and it really seems to be exacting a terrible toll on your emotions and well-being, then isn't it realistic to think seriously about planning to quit that job and take another? It's not an easy move to make but it is far from an impossibility. If you are depressed by the climate, the noise, the congestion, the struggle to commute, the crime-rate of the city where you live—a depression that compounds itself with each passing year and seems to be making you old before your time—wouldn't it be worth the mental and physical exertion it requires to move to another part of the country?

There are hundreds of such stressors which we live with, out of nothing more than a sense of resigned fatalism, waiting like children for a Fairy Godmother to drop by and change everything for the better. Perhaps such unrealistic thinking derives from the physical law of inertia that says that a body at rest tends to remain at rest. But that is applicable to inanimate objects, not people with brains and the resources to change things. I think it is better termed "the brick wall" complex. Like the stupid cat in an animated cartoon, we keep running headlong into the same hard place every day just because it is there in our rut of the old familiar rat race.

Counseling Can Definitely Relieve Stress

Far more subtle and devastating stressors are at work in many lives. But even they can be eliminated or at least dulled by actively seeking out professional counseling and advice which may help quite substantially in coping with more serious problems such as an alcoholic spouse, a deeply troubled marriage, being grossly overweight, rebellious teen-agers, aging, invalid parents, etc.

There is a natural reluctance to take such steps which somehow seem to be admitting both defeat and inviting public scrutiny of our private troubles. It is a reluctance so powerful that it keeps far too many people living in constant stress when help is often no further away than the phone directory.

But there is no shame in seeking professional help. If you think you are alone in your problem, then why have these clinics, counselors and help groups been formed? They are not just sitting there waiting for you to wake up and ask for help. They are there precisely because so many other people have the same sort of problem and have had the courage and common sense to turn to them.

The real shame is in being a passive victim to a stress than can either be eliminated or significantly reduced. In fact, and this is a promise which research backs up, just making a determined effort to set personal priorities straight and/or taking the first step toward gaining the professional knowledge and help you need, will of itself significantly reduce your stress. Why? *Because the feeling of helplessness, of seeing*

no way out, of caving in and doing nothing, is in it-
self a potent breeder of stress.

Resisting and Minimizing Stress

If a lot of needless stress can be eliminated from our
lives, and doing so is top priority, there is still no getting around the fact that to live is to experience stress.
What's worth noting at this point is that some people
actually seem to thrive on stress. Life in the fast lane
is the only one such people seem to savor. If things
get too calm they will go out and look for competition, knotty problems, business risks, even physical
danger, à la Ernest Hemingway.

Through temperament and long conditioning,
others have learned to live with prolonged stress that
would cause "melt down" in most of us. One of the
people I asked about personal relaxation techniques
is an old friend from my service days who went on
to become commanding officer of several nuclear sub-
marines. He responded: "A submarine captain is certainly under considerable stress much of the time. But
I think that, in order for him to make decisions and
take actions quickly and correctly on a round-the-clock
basis, he cannot do anything which would remove
from the front of his mind the concerns causing the
stress. Rather, during the years of his training and experience prior to attaining command, he must have
learned to live with these stresses as a 'normal' environment. In subsequent positions of responsibility,
perhaps because of this conditioning, it seems to me
that I have accepted and lived with the attendant

stresses as the normal environment without a need for looking for ways to break the stress. So, as far as I know, I have no methods to offer for your book."

Are such people immune to the destructive effects of the stress syndrome? Certainly not. But they have somehow managed to resist and cope with it far better than most of us. It may well be that they have convinced their conscious minds of the fact—repeated throughout these pages—that stress can only get to work on our physiology if we accept and perceive a stressor or a distressful situation to be harmful and disruptive. Thus, what I might immediately accept and interpret as a terribly threatening and stressful situation, they take in stride—perhaps even enjoy. My *distress* is their *eustress*.

How in the world are they able to do this? Evidently because they have prepared themselves mentally by anticipating the onset of stress, and have trained themselves to resist it, to erect defenses against it through one or another coping devices. Many such coping devices can be harmful—drinking, smoking, overeating. Baseball players help support the chewing tobacco industry; too many professional football players seem to rely on drugs. However, many more accomplish the same thing with a ritual deep breath or a wad of chewing gum. But the coping device doesn't have to be oral or even anything tangible. The best coping device is a tougher mental attitude.

That's a tactic we can all use in resisting stress that we see coming. Rather than go into a sagging, defensive, resigned mental crouch when we know a stressful event is about to envelop us (and, if you'll take

the time to notice the next time you encounter one,
your physical posture may actually mirror this in the
form of slouching shoulders, rolling eye motions, a long
sigh of resignation), we would do much better to look
it in the eye and get ready to cope with it through all
the tricks we've learned from past experience.

A most effective coping device is to say to yourself,
"I saw thing coming. I've been throught this before
and everything came out fine." Take a few deep
breaths and repeat these words: "I can handle it. It's
no big deal." As Dr. Floyd Bloom says about en-
countering potential stress: "The maximally beneficial
situation to be in is one in which one not only has
an effective coping or control response, but one in
which there's very good predictability."

Tackle stressors that you can predict head-on; why
let them get to you without a struggle to cut them
down to size. There is enough stress in life which
takes us by surprise, over which we have no control,
without caving in to that which we can anticipate, and
which we've been through before. Knowing what
you're up against is part of the information that helps
the unconscious brain find the needed solutions, to
dream up those answers and ways to cope.

The ability to resist stress, to see it as a challenge,
can be learned with practice. It may not work completely the first few times you try it. But again, taking that first step, making that first effort, is far better
than being a passive victim to runaway images of per-
secution and failure. In one sense, we all live on the
fast track these days, so we might as well learn to

swing around the corners without skidding off into the infield every time we see a rough spot or a pothole in the pavement ahead.

Of course, good physical condition, plenty of sleep, proper diet all help to maintain the ability to resist stress. But don't discount a tougher, realistic mental attitude's power to work wonders against anticipated stress. A lot of us assume that the "boss's job" must be a lot more stressful than ours. What the boss might tell you is that he got where he is by being able to resist most of that stress. After all, in many cases, he or she knows what's going to happen next because he or she has a hand in planning it—you don't.

Mental anticipation and preparation to resist stress can make a very real difference because stress is generated by the mind. It is a bit like the case of two people who take a plunge into cold water. One is out on the lake in a sailboat which suddenly jibes and overturns, throwing the person overboard. The result is flailing panic and fear. The other person sees the plight of the first, rips off his jacket and shoes and dives into the lake to help. Both are in the same cold water but the second person was prepared for the shock and knows exactly what to expect. He's going to shiver a bit when he helps pull the other person to safety, but he's going to feel good about what he did rather than experiencing any kind of distress.

Relieving Stress

The stress that we cannot eliminate and the stress we can neither resist nor minimize is "the stress of life," which we somehow must learn to live with. But living with it does not mean letting it have free run of our mental and physical house. To do so is to allow ourselves to become one of those alarming statistics, one of the 70 to 90 percent who eventually fall victim to a stress-related disease.

We now know it is not stress itself that does us in but the prolonged effect it has on our bodies. Just let it nibble away and eventually it will eat you up, at which time you will go off to the doctor or to the hospital and be treated, if possible, for a specific disorder. Stress does this to millions of people and they never know what hit them.

Belling the Tiger

Remember our friend the caveman? If he hadn't been able to drop off to sleep, his obsessive concern with the saber-toothed tiger would have driven him to nervous and bodily exhaustion. In Dr. Seyle's terms, he would have used up all his adaptive energy, all his mental and physical reserves for both fight or flight would be gone. All the tiger would have to do is amble in and gobble him up. And, as we saw, though we don't have to cope with wild predators at our door very often these days, we do have to cope with a far wider variety of stressors than did our forebear, even

HOW I RELAX

I'm not by nature, a person who has a great deal of anxiety. But at night, I take a good hot shower before I go to bed, and that helps. I also read at night for a while, and I think that helps me relax. And usually I read something not connected with my work.

I also write for diversion, but I'm not sure that fits into any successful way of relieving stress and anxiety.

It may add to it!

Paul Simon
United States Senator
Illinois

though we have much the same basic equipment for dealing with it as he did.

What we do have is a much better grasp of just how that equipment—especially our brain—works. If we have learned that under the duress of perceived distress it can trigger off an amazing number of signals which bring our nervous and physical systems to "general quarters" (a condition of battle readiness which it will sustain until countermanding orders are received from the brain), we also know how to induce the brain to issue such orders when the tiger is no longer a real threat. This can be done by using alcohol, tranquilizers and other drugs, more or less harmful. But research into effective stress relief and management has shown conclusivoly that the brain can teach itself to cope with stress without drugs.

The balance of this chapter is given over to exploring some of these non-destructive ways to cope with stress. Since every person reacts to stress differently, there can be no "best way," or universally effective formula for dealing with it. You should also be aware that many clinics and hospitals all across the country offer some version of what is usually called a "Stress Management Program." These vary in the special techniques they employ, as they do in duration—which may range from a few days to many weeks. Other programs are designed to deal with such extreme forms of stress as hysteria, panic attacks and nervous breakdowns.

Ideally, such professionally directed stress management programs seek to identify the precise nature of an individual's stress and also the particular ways in which it is afflicting the person's body. The program can thus be structured to meet that person's problems most effectively.

There is no question that such programs are the best way to go, and for people who are beset with prolonged, intense stress I certainly recommend seeking out such professionally administered stress management help at the earliest opportunity. In large cities, the Yellow Pages of the phone directory will provide leads; elsewhere your doctor or community hospital should be able to give you direction.

The basic coping methods which follow are for the great majority of people who want to do something positive to combat the effects of stress in their lives but who will probably never bring themselves to enroll in a professionally structured and administered stress management program.

As you will have gathered from reading the personal notes on relaxing scattered throughout this book, a method doesn't have to be complicated or fancy to be effective. These are simple do-it-yourself techniques, not all of which will work for any given person. Some may seem a bit strange, others quite ordinary. It is my hope that at least several of them will work for you and become "a friend indeed" in bringing you some relief from stress.

I am acutely aware that I have oversimplified scientific findings and theories of modern stress research which underlie some of these techniques. In a practical sense, it's not really necessary to understand why something works (especially something as complex as the human brain) if it does work. But in the case of stress, precisely because the brain's role both in causing and stemming stress may seem too mysterious to be credible, I wanted to include just enough theory to make the reality plausible. For many stress relief techniques to work effectively, the person employing them must be convinced that they have worked for others and that they will work for her or him.

Relaxation Is the Key

Relaxation is the opposite of tension. Nervous and muscular tension are two prime effects of stress. Prolonged stress, even after its initial "hot state" has subsided a bit, continues to keep its victims in a state of tension. They may live with such tension for so long that they finally cease to notice it and begin to accept their uptight, nervous, slightly irrascible and never quite well existence as normal. The only time they relax is at the actual moment of falling into an exhausted sleep—at which point they are unconscious and can no longer appreciate the difference. Such people—and they are legion—need to break the tension cycle, to experience both the soothing effects of relaxation and to recognize that continuous tension is not a normal state.

With relaxation, we now know that the central nervous system slows down, the heart slows, blood pressure descends, and a general sense of well-being prevails in the mind. The neural and chemical signals and excretions which are triggered by the stress syndrome are either turned off or blocked by the relaxation response's own secret weapon—endorphins, a group of hormones secreted by the brain which are possessed of wonderful tranquilizing and pain-killing powers.

Relaxation will not eliminate the cause of our stress, it will probably be retriggered by the same stressors that brought it on in the first place, but it does effectively break the tension cycle. In so doing it allows us to replenish our coping reserves, our adaptive energy, our general physical, mental and emotional health. For a while, at least, we are free of the crushing grip of stress. When it returns we are far better equipped both to resist it and endure its onslaughts of tension. And, perhaps of even greater importance, we are now aware of the fact that we've been accepting tension as a norm when it is, in fact, abnormal.

How To Induce Relaxation

Long before endorphins were ever dreamed about, let alone discovered and isolated, people were aware that relaxation and tranquility were states much to be desired. The ancient religions of the East pursued them in a variety of ways from ritual contemplation to yoga. Mystics of the West used deep meditation in pursuit of their goal of complete loss of self in "the presence of God." There is a long tradition of stories about trances so profound that no external stimuli, even pain, could penetrate to the conscious mind; of fakirs who can lie comfortably upon a cushion of sharp nails or walk on burning coals; of Buddhist monks able to suspend the laws of gravity in self-levitation.

Me, Meditate!

It's hardly surprising then, that many contemporary minds, especially skeptical minds, not only associate the very word meditation with religious zeal, but may well consider it absolutely unscientific mumbo-jumbo. Tell such people that one proven way to induce the relaxation response is through meditation and their eyes tend to glaze over. Yet more than a few of the people whose personal ways of relaxing are included in this book—busy, successful, realistic individuals all—employ meditation in one form or another to combat stress. And studies of meditation such as that conducted by researchers Wallace and Benson at Harvard back them up by showing that it can be more refreshing and energy restoring than sleep.

While the end of meditation may be deepening of religious faith for those who pursue this goal, its technique need have no religious associations whatsoever. In his response, Dr. Martin Marty, a religious man, says he uses meditational focusing as a means to drop out of consciousness for fifteen minutes once or twice a day. But the technique he details for doing so is not at all religious and it works. I've seen him put himself to sleep sitting in a chair during a break in a meeting surrounded by a room full of people.

There are, of course, many variations in techniques. Dr. Benson, who removes meditation from any religious associations, and calls it simply the "relaxation response," identified its basic elements: find a quiet place and sit comfortably with your eyes closed. Repeat a single, simple sound, or focus on a single

image and resist all extraneous thoughts. Since it is
virtually impossible to force the mind to go blank, fix-
ing on a single object, image or word enables the mind
at least to quit jumping from one thought to another
and become relatively quiet. With practice this quiet
can be sustained. Thoughts give way to a single image, or even a series of images, pictures, that run
through the mind effortlessly with remarkably refreshing results.

It may sound a bit hokey, but it works. Some people employ a "mantra" or phonetic phrase, which
they intone over and over again while breathing in
and out to its cadence—"Aahh-Soom," for instance,
with the breath coming in on the drawn out "Aahh"
and going slowly out on "Soom." Ten minutes of this,
even with your head down on an office desk after
lunch, keeping your mantra silent but spoken to yourself, and letting whatever images (not thoughts) come
as they will, can work wonders of relaxation.

Meditation by whatever name does induce relaxation. As noted, many people never try it consciously
because they think it is either religiously alien to them,
or too esoteric and complex to be employed by ordinary persons. But there is nothing weird about it—
no whirling phantasms, eerie auras, or "2001" space
light shows. It is a simple technique which produces
simple but effective results. And, whether they know
it or not, most people do meditate far more frequently
than they imagine. The kindergarten of meditation is
counting sheep in an effort to fall asleep. All the
cliches about becoming absorbed in and refreshed by
a beautiful sunset or by the sight and sound of the

breaking surf on a beach, or simply the tranquility of staring into a crackling hearth fire are really forms of meditation. The basics are there in each setting. The mind calms down and is bemused and refreshed in its own reflection and stillness.

Auto-Suggestibility

Try this on yourself some time when you're sitting around with nothing better to do. Say to yourself, "Yawn." Repeat it several times. Look at a wall or something just as unriveting. "Yawn, yawn, yawn." It's a funny word to look at and even stranger to say, but chances are in a moment or so, if you don't consciously resist the urge, you will find yourself yawning. And chances are also that if any people who aren't concentrating on some specific task or conversation see you yawning, they will soon be doing the same.

The point at hand (whether or not it worked in your case) is that the mind controls behavior, which is evident, but also that the mind is also highly susceptible to the power of suggestion. A yawn is usually an unconscious reflex triggered by the brain; in this case our mind, by the power of suggestion, caused the brain to send out the appropriate reflexive signal.

A number of modern stress management techniques exploit this openness of the brain to self-suggestibility by inducing it to send signals or to stop sending them. "Progressive Relaxation," seeks to reduce stress by making use of the relationship which seems to exist between muscular and psychological tension. If psychological stress can cause physical tension in muscles and nerves, then relaxing the nerves and muscles can also relieve psychological tension—stress. The theory, which seems to hold true in practice, is that since tension and relaxation are total opposites, one cannot exist where the other prevails. If one can succeed in totally relaxing muscles, psychological tension will necessarily disappear.

Progressive Relaxation techniques have become highly structured and are most effectively mastered in a clinical setting under the auspices of professionals. One first learns to distinguish clearly between the feeling of tenseness in a given muscle or group of muscles, and that of total relaxation in the same muscles. This is done by deliberate strong physical tensing of the muscles and then relaxing them. Getting a strong mental fix on the feeling of relaxation is the key. With practice, the relaxing signals can be "demanded" from the brain and, when the muscles are finally "happy" there will no longer be any mental stress left, either.

Like meditation, progressive relaxation is a technique that can provide a measure of real relaxation even outside the clinical setting. Again, it may sound a bit flaky to those of us who like to think in hard-edged terms, but if you have ever had a good massage by expert hands you'll admit that the feeling of warmth and well-being which floods over you in the wake of totally relaxed muscles is very real. In progressive relaxation you simply attempt to substitute your own brain for the massaging hands. My version is a radical simplification of scientific progressive relaxation, but, because the brain can, with practice, be conned into doing what you suggest, it works.

No one person's head works quite like another, so you'll have to experiment to find your own way of getting yours to respond. But basically, all you have to do is lie down in a comfortable position—one that you won't want to adjust every couple of minutes. Now mentally survey your body for tenseness and discomfort. There's definitely a knot at the back of your neck, say. And your elbow is as tight as your lower back and thigh muscles seem to be. Try to imagine how you would like them to feel. Send each area a conscious message to relax—one area at a time. Don't move on until you feel at least some improvement, some slackening of tension. Now start with your temples and neck and send the same sort of message to each identifiable part of your body (noses don't count). Do it slowly and methodically and wait for at least a trace of a result. Keep your mind totally occupied with this process. Repeat each step if necessary. You may feel like a ninny lying there talking to your buttocks and big toes, but you may also be pleasantly surprised, not only by how relaxed your muscles have in fact become (if you haven't drifted off to sleep) but by how free and easy your mind is.

Other stress management techniques which would seem to be related in some fashion to both the suggestibility and the two-way relationship between physical and mental or psychological tension include Bio-Feedback (in which sophisticated electronic instruments help pin-point and measure neurological and physical functions and reactions), hypnosis, and

Autogenic Training, which seeks to re-establish proper psychological and physiological balances or harmonies. All are in the strictly professional category, and beyond the range of do-it-yourself relaxers.

Getting Physical

By far the most common way people seek the release of relaxation is through physical activity. It may be something as fiercely energetic and exhausting as running; it may be something as passive as soaking in a hot tub. Whatever form it takes, it helps the individual to break the grip of muscular and nervous tension. And it works even at those times when one may be too busy, or simply too preoccupied, to achieve the frame of mind needed to meditate or focus sufficiently for auto-suggestion techniques to be useful.

But even though this approach to inducing relaxation is physical, its efficacy ultimately rises out of the brain. It is still related to the mental relaxation techniques, even if it works first from the "outside." If our conscious mind is too wrapped up in stress images, we can nonetheless relax our muscles and nervous system through some physical manipulation that makes the conscious mind focus on carrying out the activity and thus gets at least part of its attention off the stress. Instead of arriving at such a tranquil mental state that endorphins are released which then relax muscular tension, the relaxed muscles and nervous system somehow tell the brain that endorphins should be released.

The "high" that persistent joggers experience after

a long run is very probably caused by that flood of relaxing endorphins, which some scientists call the brain's natural opiate. With less violent exercise the same thing happens, but much more gradually, so that while there may be no sudden "high," there is simply a feeling of renewal and well-being.

In all cases the mind has been diverted to focusing on something simple and direct. The runner's brain is forced to deal with the severe demands the body is making on itself—breathing, keeping all those muscles and joints in synchronization, keeping the right balance and footing; the runner is also analyzing his or her progress, endurance, distance and time goals. It's nearly impossible to ponder deep worries or stay tense when you are running. The same thing happens—again, more gradually—to the determined walker, swimmer and cyclist.

Though it doesn't have the therapeutic cardio-vascular benefits of physical exercise, relaxation can also be induced by totally passive means. The effects of a good massage or fifteen minutes in a hot tub are so potent that muscles have little choice but to relax. Some people claim that watching television or going to the movies relaxes them. Listening—really listening—to music, especially through stereo headphones, seems to work for many. All are totally passive activities which, if they work, do so because they make the brain forget about itself for a while, not because of muscular relaxation.

Somewhere in between programmed exercise and being totally passive lies the sort of relaxation which thousands find through the catch-all term hobbies.

HOW I RELAX

I realize it may well sound flip, but I maintain that a fairly effective way of cutting down on stress is having a heart attack. Obviously, a heart attack may have been triggered by stress and is itself stressful, but my point is that if you recover—as I and hundreds of thousands have—the role of stress in your life becomes a dominant and vital concern. After such a dramatic warning, only a damn fool would continue to live as he or she did. Instead, most of us decide that a good deal of stress can and will be eliminated from our lives. From our new perspective, it no longer seems important—and certainly no reason for an uproar—because no paper was delivered today; or your are billed for something that was never received; or a gift that was promised for delivery did not arrive; or the manager of your apartment building should be working in a sausage factory if she is as nasty to the rest of the tenants as she is to you; or a relative misinterprets what you thought was a kindly action; or you made a stupid mistake in your checking account and are almost overdrawn.

Of course you cannot expect to change completely overnight, but (never forgetting that another heart attack could carry you off) before long you learn to avoid situations that formerly produced stress and, if they cannot be voided, that willpower and practice can produce far better results than might be expected from your stressful past.

Dan Herr
Publisher

There is almost always a little physical activity involved in such hobbies (working crossword puzzles
probably entails the ultimate least). But the gardener,
the knitter, the woodworker, the modelmaker, even
the ever hopeful fisherman achieve a measure of relaxation as much from having their hands busy and their
minds—or at least a part of them—occupied with familiar, pleasing tasks as they do from muscular relaxation. That, of course, may well follow and most often
does.

Get Out and Get Underway

Physical stress relief in any or all of these forms is
so simple and so effective that it is a "crime" against
oneself not to employ them. Yet a surprising number
of us fail to do so with any degree of regularity. The
more stress we feel, the more tension, the deeper we
sink into self-preoccupation and inactivity. We blame
the pace of our lives for such "criminal" neglect of
the very thing which will bring relief; but it is really
a failure of will. We all manage to make room in our
lives for what we enjoy and "getting physical" may
not be in that category.

Many people who could do so fail to establish a regular pattern of active physical exercise. You don't have
to jog (and many people shouldn't). But you can
walk—it requires no physical exam nor special equipment. A long, brisk (or at least a cut above a stroll)
walk three or four times a week is a minimum. When
it's too cold to walk, and if you can't afford, or don't
like, an exercise machine of some sort, make yourself

do ten minutes of moderate calisthenics—even if it's only bending and rotating your body. Whatever it is, do something that requires some exertion and do it regularly. Yes, it requires effort; and yes, it can get boring. But the rewards are worth it.

The point is that stress loves a sitting target. When you are in its grip and all your mental techniques for combating it have failed to work, get up out of that chair and get moving—take a walk, go swimming, get a friend to give you a rub-down, get out the tools, plant an onion, mow the grass, go fishing, knit up a storm, go bowling, fill the bathtub with warm water and get in. The knots of tension are not relieved by following the often cited Zen maxim—"Don't just do something, sit there!" The exact opposite is the case.

Circuit Breakers and Quick Fixes

Even when it's not possible to take prolonged physical action against stress, there are some quick ways to break the day's gradual tension-building patterns.

—You really don't need a cigarette in your mouth to take a moment to lean back and take a few deep breaths—more than a few.

—We take our eyes so much for granted that we tend to overwork them to death. The only way they can fight back is to communicate their discomfort through irritability or a tension headache. Give them a break at least four times a day. Close your eyes, cover them gently with your hands and put your head down on a desk or table for at least a minute.

—Once in the middle of the morning and again in the afternoon stop whatever you are doing and stand up. Stretch yourself to your full height, extend your arms straight out from your shoulders as far as they will go, arch your back, throw your head back and yawn.

—Anytime you feel like it, put your thumbs under your ears and gently massage your temples; then move your fingers up and move your scalp back and forth a few times. Then massage the knot at the base of your skull, moving over to do the same with the big muscle that extends between neck and shoulder on each side.

AFTERWORD

AS we have seen, the real secret to coping with life in the 80s is to rid ourselves of unjustified, unrealistic guilt; eliminate all unnecessary stress; resist and minimize what cannot be eliminated, and manage what's left with every means at our disposal.

The most dangerous enemy is not the one we see lined up across the battlefield in ordered rows, shouting threats and rattling sabers. The worst enemy is the one who takes us by ambush, the one we don't even know is there until it is too late to fight back. That's why simply becoming aware of the unseen but potentially lethal forces of guilt and stress is of itself a tremendous advantage in combatting them.

We should all know by now that unless we have fallen prey to a bacterium, virus or other true physiological illness, the squeezing tension, the sweaty hands, the wrenching spasms in our guts, our pounding temples, and our total obsession with worry is not coming out of the air, or from something we ate. It's coming out of our own mind, our own sense of guilt, our self-generated reaction to stress.

It's my hope that this book not only has helped to drive this realization home, but that it will assist you in your personal quest, not just to cope with guilt and stress, but to enjoy life to the fullest in a hectic, ever-changing, but still endlessly fascinating, rewarding world.